Praise from others for *Spirit Soi*

"I proudly endorse David Reid [...] a recently retired Navy Chaplain and having served on four different Navy combatant vessels with four overseas deployments, including deployments to the Persian Gulf, I identify with every word David reveals in his journal. Not only do I know David as a fellow Navy Chaplain, but I also know him to be a humble man of great character, and I call him friend. *Spirit Soundings* is a window allowing us to see David's conviction of faith and his commitment to serve God's people in the Sea Services. If you are a greenhorn (little or no experience) on the matters of life onboard a Navy combatant ship, this book will present a vivid, day-to-day, summary of a then young Chaplain's spiritual life during his first shipboard assignment. If you are an old salt, like me, you will be touched by the author's ability to paint the picture with imaginative words and candor; so much so, that as I read this journal, it caused me to laugh, cry, and pray all in one sitting. The stories are simple, yet deeply immersed in the Eternal.

"The message within this book is simple: "In the beginning, the Spirit of God hovered upon the surface of the waters..." and today each of us can still encounter God there. Be inspired far beyond par! Read it and expect the unexpected."

-Captain Brenda BradleyDavila, CHC, USN (Ret.)
Colorado Springs, Colorado

It has been my privilege to know David Reid Brown and his family since 2010. Dave is a man of God that I respect, one whom hears from God and has the courage to be God's messenger. I am certain that *Spirit Soundings* is going to challenge each person to a renewed sense of openness to the voice of God. *Spirit Soundings* will show you that God is always speaking and directing by his Spirit and it will challenge you to expect to hear from Him."

-Rev. Andy Casper
Lead Pastor, South County Church
Lorton, Virginia

Spirit Soundings provides a unique and first-hand view of military chaplaincy yet, I believe, also has an appeal to the un-churched / seekers, especially young people who may feel life circumstances are pushing them beyond their own limits and resources, and are seeking God actively or unknowingly. In *Spirit Soundings,* David Reid Brown gives us the result of "sailing into a hazardous world" as a newly deployed Navy Chaplain. These pages offer a spiritually mature, sometimes striking, often moving account of a man of God called to offer comfort and counsel to young men and women at sea. It's a compelling, deeply honest and wise read.

-Rev. Denise Mosher
Salem, Oregon

Through *Spirit Soundings,* Chaplain David Reid Brown introduces readers to the exciting reality that God is at work in every thing that happens. David is a man of great spiritual fervor, who exemplifies the high ideals of Christian living and giving. I have known him since he entered the ministry twenty-three years ago, when I served as the pastor of an AME church in Roanoke, VA. Knowing him has been an inspiration to me because of who he is and I consider him to be my 'Best Friend and Brother'.

-Rev. Frank W. Saunders
Clayton, North Carolina

Dear Congresswoman Gabbard,

May the reading of this book bring hope and inspiration to your life.

Sincerely,

David Reid Brown

SPIRIT SOUNDINGS

Volume I: Sailing into a Hazardous World

A CHAPLAIN'S JOURNAL OF LIFE AT SEA

DAVID REID BROWN

DEDICATION

To Almighty God:

The One who makes all such stories possible.

ACKNOWLEDGEMENTS

I would like to thank the families of Information Systems Technician Second Class (Surface Warfare) Kris R. Bishundat and Machinist Mate Fireman Patrick D. White for allowing me to share the story of your son, brother, and Sailor.

Dr. Larry Keefauver, for his invaluable work and wisdom and all it contributed to getting this book published.

Master Chief Machinist Mate (Surface Warfare) Scott Maretich, who refreshed my memory of and fondness for Steam Engineering and "Snipes".

Mrs. Tina Martinez, for her assistance with the portions of the book that required Spanish to English translation.

They took soundings and found that the water
was a hundred and twenty feet deep.
A short time later they took soundings again
and found it was ninety feet deep.
Fearing that we would be dashed against the rocks,
they dropped four anchors from the stern
and prayed for daylight.
(Acts 27:28-29)

TABLE OF CONTENTS

Preface xi

1–Beginnings (October 12, 2000) 13

2–Check-In Day (October 28, 2000) 16

3–Reporting for Duty (October 30, 2000) 19

4–Underway (October 30, 2000). 23

5–Burial at Sea (November 01, 2000) 29

6–Port Everglades, Florida (November 04, 2000) 35

7–Habitat for Humanity (November 05, 2000) 38

8–Worship Service at Sea (November 12, 2000) 41

9–Naval Weapons Station Yorktown (November 14, 2000) 48

10–Standown (January 2001). 51

11–Work-Ups (February 2001). 54

12–Antigua (March 15, 2001) 70

13–North for Norfolk (April 01, 2001) 92

14–Fleet Week (May 18, 2001). 109

15–Fireman White (July 08, 2001). 150

16–Joint Task Force Exercise (July 30, 2001) .157

17–Cape Hatteras 194

18–9/11 (September 11, 2001) 209

19–Mission: Morehead City (September 12, 2001) 215

20–Standown: Return to Norfolk (September 13, 2001) 220

Epilogue 225

PREFACE

People are my details. Discerning and then attending to the needs of others have always been my center of gravity. Through my professional career, first as a civilian pastor and most recently as a Navy Chaplain, I have embraced the fact that I was created to be a care provider. Many of my colleagues build programs that meet the broad range of needs in our institution while others build policies and procedures that govern our conduct and allow for the efficient flow of administration. As for me,

I build people.

Here is how: *God took my innate "wiring" and placed it on a career path through which it could be used to bring out what is best in others.*

My mother told me one thing before I departed for my first tour as a Navy Chaplain: "Write it down!" I suppose that she sensed some very unique experiences in my future would be worth recording. However, I never took her advice. I was just too enamored with the sensory aspects— sights, sounds, and sojourn— of the experience to be bothered with "pen and paper." So, all of my experiences during my first tour of duty at Twentynine Palms, California and the following one at Great Lakes, Illinois, now exist in ever-fading memories.

My change of heart came upon accepting orders to my first ship assignment to the USS SHREVEPORT (LPD-12). I suppose that every Navy

Chaplain's dream is to go to sea; it took me nearly six years to fulfill mine. From my very first day aboard ship, I had this overwhelming sense that this experience was going to be very special—even remarkable—thus, worthy of recording. Hats off to a mother's wisdom!

At this writing, there are over 800 Active Duty and Reserve Component Navy Chaplains, each one with the ability to pen a far more interesting story. Nonetheless, this one is mine; it is a junior chaplain's chronicle of his initial experience at sea.

My prayer is that God would use this account to open
or deepen His relationship with you.

- David Reid Brown

-1-

BEGINNINGS
Sailing into a hazardous world

12 October 2000

There were only a few more items to pack into my large luggage bag sitting on the bed in the guestroom and then we would be ready to make our trip from my in-laws' house to our new home in Chesapeake, Virginia. My wife was in the living room attending to our four-month-old son. My mother-in-law came into the room and announced, "David, they have just bombed some ship over there in the Gulf. Come and take a look. It's on CNN."

Stunned at the news, I stopped packing and followed her down the hallway and into the den. My wife picked up our son and came down shortly afterwards. My eyes were immediately fixed on the bottom of the screen where the captions were posted.

"USS COLE Attacked In Aden, Yemen…4 Dead, 11 Others Missing."

I sighed and shook my head in anger and disbelief.

"Oh, no!" my wife exclaimed, voicing her protest and shock at the news. The pictures said it all—a gaping hole blown out from the side of the ship. The steel around the hole was charred and the water at the surface was littered with debris and suds from firefighters' foam. My immediate reaction was to think about the others who were missing and probably killed in the attack. However, it was much too early to tell.

The newsflash of this attack could not have come at a more inopportune time. I had just accepted a set of orders to the USS SHREVEPORT (LPD-12) in Norfolk, Virginia. These were my first "sea duty" orders, but my third set of orders since becoming a Navy Chaplain in the summer of 1995. As I think about it, even that moment was filled with uncertainty and apprehension. I had been an ordained minister in the African Methodist Episcopal Church for four years, the last three of which were as a pastor in southwestern Virginia.

Being a pastor was challenging and rewarding work. During that time, I met a Navy Recruiter, who was also a chaplain. He showed me all the typical brochures and flyers that I had expected from someone in his position. Then he surprised me with an offer to spend a week at the Naval Station in Norfolk to observe the various settings in which Navy Chaplains serve. It sounded interesting; I "took the bait." I finished the week excited about the prospects of ministry that the Navy had to offer.

We were still focusing on CNN when my mother-in-law interrupted and suggested, "David, do you think you will need to call in and report?"

"No," I answered confidently. "Nobody knows that I am here."

Check-in for duty was at least three days away. Although I was in the area, they had plenty of chaplains able to respond to the crisis.

In a situation like that, chaplains are utilized in a couple of ways. First, they can accompany a Casualty Assistance Call Officer or CACO (Kay-ko) to the residence of the next of kin for the injured, killed or missing service member. Then they are on hand to provide pastoral care to the immediate family members. A casualty assistance notification is always conducted in the formal Service Dress uniform. The CACO and the chaplain walk right up to the front door and deliver the message about the service member. It is the one sight that all military members understand and all family members dread. Throughout the military, the sight of anyone coming to your door in a Service Dress uniform, beside oneself, always means bad news.

It was late and we were all tired when we arrived in Chesapeake. Our son had slept most of the way and was still asleep in his infant car seat. It took a while for my wife and me to unpack the car. I plopped down on the sofa, and as was my custom, I reached for the remote to do some channel surfing. The news of the attack was now being covered all over the three major networks as well as CNN. The death toll had risen. Unfortunately, they were now counting the missing among the dead. From the kitchen, my wife asked, "Anymore about the COLE?"

"Yeah. The missing persons are being reported as dead."

She walked in from the kitchen and saw the images of the hole in the hull and the charred steel that surrounded it.

"Hmmm!" she expressed with concern. "What does this mean, Honey?"

I guess I was tired because my answer was a bit short, "Honey, there is no way I will be involved in this thing! Nobody knows that I am here, and they won't know until I have checked in on Monday. It is a tough situation, but I know they have got it covered. There is no way I will be involved."

"Okay! Okay!" she said with acceptance. She turned away and headed back to the kitchen. I let out an exhausted sigh and was about to change the channel when the caption read:

"COLE Attacked In Yemen, 17 Dead…."

"Man, what a mess!" I thought in disgust.

"No way I will be a part of this. No way."

God was listening and He had a plan. His ways are higher than ours.

2

CHECK-IN DAY

Ministry at a moment's notice

28 October 2000

Two weeks had passed since the attack on COLE. The grieving continued while memorial services and funerals were taking place. The Naval Station in Norfolk hosted the largest memorial service with national dignitaries present: the President, Secretary of Defense, Chief of Naval Operations, Commander-in-Chief of the Atlantic Fleet, and the Chief of Navy Chaplains, to name a few. Thousands of sailors, family members, and the general public also attended.

The service was very poignant. Many were sobbing quietly, some openly in a communion of solace. People who serve in uniform understand that they may be called to give their lives in the line of duty. They accept that fact and carry on. Whenever this kind of sacrifice is necessary, it is neither welcome nor convenient.

Before I checked in with SHREVEPORT, I had to make a courtesy In-Call with my Supervisory Chaplain. I would be working for Commander, Amphibious Group Two (PHIBGRU2) located at the Naval Amphibious Base in Little Creek, Virginia. SHREVEPORT was one of several ships that comprised PHIBGRU2, even though most of those were docked at the Naval Station in Norfolk piers. I was generally familiar with the location of the command building and remembered that the chaplain's office was on the third deck.

My predecessor aboard SHREVEPORT was my host escort for the visit. He briefed me on what to expect from the command chaplain and politely reminded me that, "You work for the ship's CO." That was good advice for someone who was not familiar with an independent sea duty billet like SHREVEPORT. The custom for junior chaplains serving on a staff was to pay special attention to the senior chaplain even though the commanding officer signed the fitness report. I had done an independent billet before with the Marines in California, so I knew the ropes. Still, it was advice well taken.

We entered the office and made the customary greetings to the Religious Program Specialist (RP) seated at the front desk. An RP was primarily responsible for providing the chaplain with administrative, sacramental, and force protection support. The command chaplain was expecting us so he did not bother to wait until we reached his inner office to greet us. With a hearty handshake he said, "Welcome Aboard! Come in and sit down! Great to see you here, David!" He was definitely charged up. It is good to see that enthusiasm in a command chaplain. After several tours, junior chaplains sometimes notice that seniors seem to lose their "fire." No problem of that in this office!

We took our seats and I prepared for the usual "Twenty Questions" like: *Wife's name? Any kids? Are you settled? Where have you served? What is your denomination?* But the next words out of his mouth were not interrogative at all.

"Okay, David, you have got three burials at sea ceremonies to do once you report for duty."

Hello! I thought. *Who died? Three sailors! Maybe there was a car accident over the weekend?*

"Two of the burials are retired service members—one Coast Guard, one Navy. The third is a Sailor from the USS COLE. Now, David, that one from the COLE will be a high visibility event. There may even be some press coverage. You need to have things squared away!"

In the Christian life, there is something known as "The Conviction of the Holy Spirit." It is the moment in believers' life when they unmistakably sense the immediate presence of God or hear His voice.

God's Spirit can warn of danger;
or, reveal that you're about to stray from the "straight and narrow path."
The Spirit's conviction can point out improper words or actions,
which can "boomerang" and figuratively hit you right in the face.

At that moment, the conviction was heavy upon me and my heart began to sink into my stomach. Every reference that I made back in Richmond and at home concerning "No Way" was pummeling my conscience. *The Lord does this every so often to remind his children that he is still in control— of everything*!

The PHIBGRU2 Chaplain went over some other details concerning the burials and I quickly made some mental notes about them. He did end up asking maybe four or five of the "Twenty Questions." He offered his phone number, email, and requested a copy of the ship's Officer Social Roster.

The meeting concluded, taking less than twenty minutes. I left his office still stunned that I would be "On Point" for the burials. This was an instance where God made ministry happen at a moments notice. At first, He catches you by surprise then surprisingly equips you to do His will.

3

REPORTING FOR DUTY
The "New Kid on the Block"

30 October 2000

The business day for shore commands usually began at 0730. I carried that assumption as I traveled along Interstate 64 to the exit for the naval station. I remembered the general configuration of the piers from my orientation week back in 1993. The command chaplain told me that was moored at the "South Wall, Starboard side to," meaning the ship was docked at the very end of all the piers with the right side of the ship adjacent to the pier.

I passed the guard's shack and drove down toward the South Wall. Sure enough, there it was. The first thing one notices about a ship is its profile from the stern (back of the ship). It had a long, flat Flight Deck primarily used by helicopters. Directly beneath that was a cavernous space called the Well Deck, where all amphibious operations took place. All decks and compartments above the Flight Deck seemed to be compressed forward into an inclining stack starting with the Boat Deck (a.k.a. Smoke Deck), the Bridge Deck, and finally the Signal Bridge. One could go higher on the ship to reach its RADAR and the top of the mast, which extended about eighty feet above the Signal Bridge.

SHREVEPORT was known as an Austin Class Amphibious Transport Dock (LPD) and the twelfth ship in this class. This class of ship falls into the unofficial category of "Gator-Freighter." It was designed to embark Marines and their ground, air, and logistical support assets, and then transport them through ship-to-shore movements. Some of her sister ships, like the NASHVILLE, TRENTON, and PONCE were also home ported at the Naval Station in Norfolk.

I located a space to park in the lot across from the ship, grabbed my briefcase, and headed for the brow. I was wearing my Service Dress Blue uniform, which was appropriate anytime of the year but especially for conducting official business. On each sleeve of my jacket was a single gold cross, informing all the sailors that I was the chaplain. SHREVEPORT was experiencing a gap in coverage since the previous chaplain had detached from the ship several months earlier.

Still walking towards the brow, I began to brush up on my shipboard etiquette, especially coming aboard ship. The last time I practiced coming aboard ship was five years ago during a class exercise at the Naval Chaplain's Basic Course in Newport, Rhode Island. I did not want to seem rusty so I kept reciting the procedure as I walked: "When you get to the top of the brow, salute the National Ensign (flag) and then request permission to come aboard."

I reached the brow, saluted the Ensign, and proceeded to the Quarterdeck where I was met by the Petty Officer-of-the-Watch:

"Permission to come aboard?"

"Come aboard, Sir!" replied the Petty Officer. "We have been expecting you."

Nice to be noticed, I thought.

"Sir, do you know how to get to your stateroom?"

"Uh, not really," I said.

Immediately, the Petty Officer summoned one of the messengers over to where we were standing.

"Hey! Take the chaplain to his stateroom," he ordered.

"This way, Sir," the messenger said as he led the way.

"Thanks, Petty Officer."

"No problem, Sir."

We proceeded up the ladder and inside the skin of the ship. The passageways were narrow and just high enough so that I would not scrape my head with every step. My stateroom was in "Officer's Country," one of the two decks above the Main Deck designated as officer berthing.

The messenger led me to the blue hatch of my stateroom and said, "Here you go, Sir. Do you need me to open it up?"

"No. They gave me a key the other day."

"Is this your first time aboard a ship?" he asked.

"Yes."

"Do you know if you get sea sick?"

"I am not sure. I have never been to sea," I responded.

"Okay. Well, have a good one, Sir!"

"You, too, Shipmate."

As I dismissed him I realized that I needed to check in with the Executive Officer (XO) to get situated and I had no clue where to find him.

I poked my head outside of the hatch and called to the messenger, "Hey, do you know where I can find the XO?"

"Yes, Sir. All of the officers are in the Wardroom attending the Navigation Brief."

"How do I get there?" I asked.

"I will show you a short cut."

I left my briefcase and cover in my stateroom and followed him down the passageway. He opened the door, which led into the Wardroom Galley. It seemed that they had just finished breakfast because the Mess Specialists were washing up the dishes and storing utensils.

The messenger opened the door leading into the Wardroom. The officers were seated and assembled at the tables. They seemed to be right in the middle of the brief. I would have preferred not to interrupt, but the door was wide open and I was in my Service Dress Blue Uniform so inconspicuousness went by the wayside.

For a moment, all eyes were on my entrance into the Wardroom. I quickly spotted an empty seat in the back and took my place. There was an Ensign at the front pointing to a chart giving his brief to the captain. I sat quietly and observed. Every few moments various officers would look back and eyeball me. I was the new kid on the block, even if I was the chaplain. I could just imagine what they were thinking. "What is this guy going to be like?" was probably the consensus.

After the brief concluded, I met up with the XO. He briefed me on the plan for the two wakes that afternoon. Family members for the two deceased sailors would be present. I was tasked with giving a very brief memorial message and prayer for both. The ceremonies would take place in the Well Deck of the ship in what is known as Upper Vehicle Storage ("Upper V").

At about 1230, the first of the three caskets arrived. It was taken from the hearse, up the side brow, through Side Port 1, and brought into Upper V. The pallbearers were in full military dress, three Petty Officers on each side of the casket with a Chief Petty Officer escorting from behind. Two of the three caskets were placed in the Cargo Elevator while the last was laid in state beside the podium that I would use for his memorial service. The first family arrived aboard ship about ten minutes before the service. They had the opportunity to meet the Captain, XO, and Command Master Chief (CMC). After their greeting, I introduced myself and escorted them to their seats.

The first service began promptly at 1300. I gave an invocation, read an appropriate portion of scripture, and offered remarks based upon it. The family members sat quiet and sullen throughout the service. The shipmate we were memorializing was a retired Sailor and Coast Guardsmen. The second service followed in the same manner at 1400. There would not be a memorial for the Sailor from the COLE. Rather, an appropriate burial at sea ceremony would be conducted.

-4-

UNDERWAY
I'm finally a "Sailor"

30 October 2000

I t had never been our custom as a family to have long, drawn out, good-byes when I had to deploy. We started this when I first deployed to Japan from Twentynine Palms, California. My wife dropped me off at the designated location where the Marines and sailors would board the buses to the airport.

A hug, a kiss, and that was about it.

We just knew that lingering longer at that moment would not delay the inevitable, rather, it would make it that much more difficult. So, when I had to get underway the next day, she parked the car long enough to go through our ritual. The difference was that now I had a "little man" in a car seat to whom I had to say "good-bye."

Once aboard, I wanted to witness the process of getting underway. I knew that the Pilot House was the place to be. It was not too hard to retrace my steps to my stateroom. I had no idea how to get to the Pilot House, and I was not too proud to ask for directions. Once I reached the hatch, I could hear a buzz of activity on the other side. I opened the door slowly and I am glad that I did. The room was filled with sailors: the CO & XO, officers and enlisted, and one civilian—the Harbor Pilot (I learned later). They were all doing *something*: scanning the harbor with binoculars, passing information on sound-powered phones, or "clicking" walkie-talkies. Some were manning the wheel, chart tables, scopes, pacing and peering over the bridge wings to check clearances—everyone had a specific job to do. On one hand, I marveled at the dynamic synergy of all personnel working together for a singular purpose. On the other, it was sensory overload. There was so much going on and I did not have a clue or a clear purpose about what to do. So I played the "wallflower" standing in a small corner at the back of the Pilot House, taking care to stay out of the way.

"Boatswain Mate-of-the-Watch, call, 'Underway!'" the Officer-of-the-Deck barked out to the Sailor standing next to me.

"Aye, Aye, Sir!" he replied. He turned, unhooked a small microphone, and gave it a click.

"UNDERWAY! SHIFT COLORS!"

His command, heard inside and outside of the ship, was immediately followed by a long and resounding blast of the ship's whistle.

So that is it, I thought. *That is the 1MC!* Everyone in my naval orientation, from recruiters in Richmond to Basic Course instructors in Rhode Island, spoke of the sacred privilege of delivering the Evening Prayer at Sea over the 1MC. I considered the opportunity to pray over the ship each night as God's moment to reach the crew.

With the guidance of the Harbor Pilot and the assistance of two tugboats, we began to pull out of our mooring position and slowly turn to starboard (right). I stepped out of the crowded commotion of the Pilot House and onto the starboard bridge wing to get a better, open-air view. Slowly and steadily, we proceeded past other destroyers, cruisers, and aircraft carriers docked at the piers. The winds picked up as we turned slightly to starboard.

I closed my eyes for a moment so all I could pick up was the sound and sensation of the wind on my face.

I began to listen for the Lord's presence.

We proceeded out of the channel, passed the Hampton Roads Bridge Tunnel, crossed the Chesapeake Bay Bridge Tunnel, viewed the lighthouses at Fort Story and Cape Henry, left Lynnehaven in our wake, and turned starboard heading towards open water. After more than five years of waiting—first three "baking" in Twentynine Palms, the next two-and-a-half "freezing" in Great Lakes—I was finally at sea. With the ship now in open water, I could feel it perform a gentle rock and sway. I stayed outside long enough to watch the Virginia Beach waterfront begin to disappear into the horizon. I was grateful that this underway period was a brief one. I would be only a couple of weeks at sea then home before Thanksgiving and in port through the New Year.

Early Evening

I knew that I had to prepare my first Evening Prayer at Sea, but wondered, *What should I say?* I had seen many excerpts of prayers back in chaplain's school in Newport, Rhode Island. Now I was on my own to compose one.

I took a moment, bowed and prayed in my stateroom before I jotted anything down:

Gracious Lord, grant me the words that you would have me use to reach the crew this evening. I release my talents, gifts, and abilities to you that they may be used to your glory, in Jesus' name, Amen.

2150

Pilot House

I returned to the spot in the Pilot House where I began earlier that day. Only now, it was pitch dark outside. The only way I could see anything was due to the ambient light emanating from RADAR scopes and the low-level red lights at the chart table and the desk in front of the 1MC. I had to identify the Boatswain Mate-of-the-Watch so that I could check in and let him know I was present.

"Good Evening, Sir!" he said.

"Good Evening," I replied.

"Sir, do you know how to use the 1MC?" he asked.

"No, please show me," I said.

"It is simple. In about three minutes I will announce, 'Tattoo...Stand by for the Evening Prayer.' I will hand you the 1MC, just key the microphone with this button on top and then you are ready to pray. Easy enough?"

"Yes. Everyone will be able to hear me?" I asked.

"Yes, Sir, the whole entire ship," he said.

"Wow!" I said under my breath.

"Okay, Sir. You have about two minutes," he said.

"Okay. Thanks."

Lord, God, this is your sacred moment.
Please speak to the heart of the crew, in Jesus' name, Amen.

"About sixty seconds, Sir," said the Boatswain Mate.

"Okay."

The Boatswain Mate cleared the desk of logbooks, pens, and paperwork so that I had a clear space on which to place my written prayer. I had the prayer concealed in a folder until the moment that I would recite it.

The Boatswain Mate-of-the-Watch took one last look at the clock on the bulkhead, turned and said, "Officer-of-the-Deck, Tattoo."

"Sound Tattoo!" he replied from the darkness.

"Ready, Sir?"

"Ready," I replied.

The Boatswain Mate unhooked the microphone, brought it to his mouth and said,

"*TATTOO, TATTOO! LIGHTS OUT IN FIVE MINUTES! STAND BY FOR THE EVENING PRAYER.*"

I placed the folder on the desk and opened it under the illumination of the red light. The Boatswain Mate handed me the microphone and I began to pray.

Let us pray

O Gracious God,
SHREVEPORT is underway again and we thank you for all
hands on board.
This training evolution seeks to build the confidence and competence of the
entire crew. We want to be ready when our nation calls.
"No Shore Too Distant," is our motto and a claim we are capable of backing
up. Yet we realize there are times in our lives when we cannot see beyond
the horizon.

We are unsure of what the future may hold.
Our lives are in your hands. Grant us your Peace.
We have left behind those whom we love and all that is familiar and dear.
Though not present, we carry them close to our hearts tonight
and reflect in our private moments how truly precious they are to us.
Keep them within your care until we return.
Their lives are in your hands. Cover them with your love.
Remind us of our responsibility to watch out for our shipmates.
Indeed, we are our "brothers' keepers."
Help us to ask the right questions, go the extra mile,
and pay attention to detail.
For we all desire a safe journey.

Our lives are in your hands. Sustain us by your grace.
As we turn to you, forgive our sin and have mercy on us.
As we trust in you, protect our lives and guide us by your Spirit.
As we turn to you, renew our hearts and make us clean.
As we trust in you, fill us with hope and increase our faith.

O Gracious God, this is our prayer; this is our plea.
Our lives are in your hands.
Amen.

When I finished, the sailors on Watch were silent, manning their posts as they did before I started.

"Thanks, Boats," I said handing him the microphone.

"Thank you, Sir!" he said hanging it back up.

There was no way to tell how it was received, no "Amen!" or a pat on the back like I was used to back in the parish. I took a moment to let my pulse settle before I left the Pilot House for the night.

"Officer-of-the-Deck," said Boats.

"Officer-of-the-Deck, Aye!" he responded.

"TAPS"?

"Sound TAPS!" he ordered.

Boats picked up the 1MC once again and said,

"TAPS, TAPS, LIGHTS OUT! ALL HANDS TURN TO YOUR BUNKS. MAINTAIN SILENCE ABOUT THE DECKS. TAPS!"

My first day underway as a Sailor was "under my belt". I thought it went pretty well, especially, the prayer. Listening to the Lord's voice throughout the day made all the difference.

BURIAL AT SEA

Freedom isn't free

01 November 2000
Rehearsal

I had never conducted a burial at sea ceremony so I relied heavily on the knowledge and experience of my assistant, RP1 Paul Bates. As part of the First Class Petty Officer's Mess, he made all necessary connections within the command through reaching out to his colleagues. He took care of all administrative and logistical matters that made the rehearsal run so well. Most importantly, I really appreciated his patience with my inexperience—walking me through the program twice, detailing the positioning of personnel on the Flight Deck—he was superb! I began to realize that we were going to have a good working relationship.

02 November
Ceremony

The burial at sea ceremony went off without a hitch! For the record, I decided to draft and submit an article about the ceremony to my Church's newspaper, "The Christian Recorder," so that members of my denomination could have a glimpse of the honor, solemnity, and dignity that goes into such a ceremony.

BURIAL AT SEA
By LT David R. Brown, CHC, USN

The following is an account of the Burial-at-Sea ceremony for a Sailor who was tragically killed along with 16 other sailors when a terrorist bomb exploded alongside of the USS COLE on October 12, 2000.

The Burial-at-Sea ceremony is one of the highest honors that the Navy can bestow on a fallen Sailor. At the request of his family, this honor was rendered to their beloved son, husband, and father. The ceremony took place aboard the USS SHREVEPORT stationed in Norfolk, Virginia.

02 November 2000
8:40 am

Off the coast of South Carolina, the USS SHREVEPORT headed into position to commence the burial at sea ceremony. Sunny skies and calm seas prevailed as the participants moved into formation on the Flight Deck. Members present were the Commanding Officer (Captain), Executive Officer, Chaplain, Honor Guard, Firing Detail, Pallbearers, and the uncle of the fallen Sailor.

Once everyone was in place, the Officer-of-the-Deck passed the word over the ships' intercom: "ALL HANDS BURY THE DEAD." He then slowed the ship to bare steerageway, and ordered the flag to be flown half-mast.

8:42 am

The Command Master Chief gave an order, "SHIP'S COMPANY, AT-TEN-TION!" All participants snapped smartly to the position of attention as the pallbearers brought the flag-draped casket of Petty Officer Saunders towards the middle of the Flight Deck. They proceeded, making synchronized steps—first, left foot, then right, then left again—until they reached the appointed position next to the Honor Guard. The Command Master Chief gave the order *"PARADE REST!"* and at once the participants relaxed from their position of attention to fold their arms behind their backs.

8:45 am

The Chaplain read several scriptures that were deemed appropriate for the occasion. *"God is our refuge and strength, a very present help in the time of trouble. Therefore, we will not fear, though the earth does change, and though the mountains are shaken into the heart of the seas."* He continued with a question: *"What shall separate us from the love of God?"* And concluded by reciting its answer: *"For I am persuaded that neither death, nor life…nor things present, nor things to come…nor anything else in all creation, will be able to separate us from the love of God in Christ Jesus our Lord."*

"LET US PRAY," the Chaplain announced, with all hands bowing their heads accordingly. All hands then recited *"The Lord's Prayer"* in unison led by the Chaplain.

8:50 am

At the conclusion of the prayer, the Command Master Chief once again ordered, *"SHIP'S COMPANY, AT-TEN-TION! HAND SALUTE!"* All participants came to attention and rendered a hand salute to the departed. The Firing Detail, comprised of United States Marines, was given an order by their Gunnery Sergeant, *"FIRING SQUAD, PRE-SENT ARMS!"* In tandem, the Marines brought their rifles to the ready position in front of their chests and awaited further orders. The pallbearers lifted the casket from the Flight Deck and proceeded to carry it to the edge of the ship, settling it down at the brink of the ammunition chute. The Chaplain read the Committal, *"Unto Almighty God, we commend the soul of our brother departed, and we commit his body to the deep…"* After the flag was lifted, the pallbearers tilted the casket and allowed it to slide from the ship into the sea. A radio message was sent to the Officer-of-the-Deck to mark the exact time and location of the burial. The Firing Detail was given the command, *"OR-DER ARMS!"* at which they placed their rifles at their left shoulders. The Command Master Chief then addressed the participants, *"PA-RADE REST!"*

8:55 am

The Navy Hymn, "Eternal Father, Strong to Save," was played in the background as the Captain read the Benediction. All heads remained bowed until "AMEN," marking the end of the Benediction. "SHIP'S COMPANY, AT-TENTION! HAND SALUTE!" the Command Master Chief ordered for the last time. The Marine Gunnery Sergeant gave his Marines this order, "FIRING DETAIL, FIRE THREE VOLLEYS!" The Firing Detail, positioned at the end of the Flight Deck facing the sea, had a moment's pause before they heard, "READY," their rifles pointed to the sky. "AIM," they placed a keen eye on the barrel and a firm grip on their weapon. "FIRE!" The first shot cracked through the morning air. "AIM...FIRE!" The second shot rang out reviving the echo of the first. "AIM...FIRE!" The third volley completed the order that was given. All hands remained at attention as a lone bugler played "Taps," the most poignant, closing tribute to honor the fallen. The Firing Detail as well as the Honor Guard secured their weapons and concluded their salutes respectively.

9:03 am

With all hands still at attention, the pallbearers began to encase the flag that once covered the casket, folding it hand-over-hand into a tightly bound triangle. The flag was presented to the Chief Master-at-Arms, who then slowly marched towards the captain. The captain rendered a hand salute before receiving the flag, turned to his right and presented it to his uncle that it would remain in its rightful place with the family. A radio signal was given to the Officer-of-the-Deck who in turn had the word passed, "SECURE FROM BURIAL AT SEA!"

As I observed his uncle receive his nephew's flag, one thought became abundantly clear,

Freedom isn't free.
It must be purchased through sacrifice
and usually understands one price—
the shedding of blood.

This Sailor, as well as the others who perished aboard the USS COLE, willingly sacrificed their lives in service to their country upholding its most precious ideal of freedom. This principle permeates Christian theology. Jesus once declared, "The Son of Man came to serve and not to be served and *to give his life* as a ransom for many."[1]

My Brothers and Sisters, let us never take for granted the liberty we enjoy as Americans because it has required the enormous and, at times, continuous struggle to preserve it. Remember to pray for the men and women of the Armed Forces for their willingness to place themselves in harm's way to protect our liberty and way of life. Finally, we as Christians should never relieve ourselves from the obligation we have to praise God for the eternal freedom we have so graciously received from Jesus Christ, our Lord.

David R. Brown

Lieutenant, U.S. Navy

Chaplain Corps

"TATTOO, TATTOO! LIGHTS OUT IN FIVE MINUTES! STAND BY FOR THE EVENING PRAYER!"

Let us pray.

Thank you, Lord, for clear skies, warm breezes and calm seas.
Thank you for such a beautiful day.
The weather you provided served to heighten the crew's expectation
for Liberty in Fort Lauderdale.
After working so hard underway, Liberty is always a good thing.
Thank you for the perfect setting for the burial at sea ceremony.
We took time out to bestow the highest honor upon shipmates
who have gone to their eternal rest.
This ceremony was of particular significance
because it taught a special lesson: his death reminds us that freedom isn't free.

---

[1] Matthew 20:28

It must be purchased and paid for, usually with one price,
the shedding of blood.
His passing, as well as the others from the COLE,
has made our liberty that much more precious and sweet this evening.
Let us not take it for granted.
Again, thank you, Lord, for a beautiful day,
a sacred moment, and a safe journey to Florida.
Amen.

-6-

PORT EVERGLADES, FLORIDA

The search for a Liberty Buddy

04 November 2000

We arrived in Florida in the late afternoon of 03 November 2000. About forty-five minutes after we moored, the officers were presented with a port brief in the Wardroom, where several representatives from the port authority and local sponsors provided information about Fort Lauderdale and the surrounding area. One-by-one they addressed us offering tips on the best beaches, transportation, restaurants, shopping, sporting events, and Community Relations (COMREL) projects.

The two things I was interested in were the University of Miami vs. Virginia Tech football game and the home building project offered by Habitat for Humanity. The game was significant since Tech was ranked number two in the nation. Also, I used to be a pastor out in the "Hokie Territory" of southwestern Virginia. As for Habitat for Humanity, it seemed like a good service project of which to be a part.

It was game day but I had one problem: No Liberty Buddy. The captain had a policy that every crew member—officer and enlisted—had to have a Liberty Buddy in order to get off the ship. I did not know any of the officers well enough to ask them to be my buddy. Besides, who wants to hang with the chaplain on Liberty? Liberty was supposed to be fun—bars, nightclubs, drinking—and having the chaplain as your Liberty Buddy was like having your mom or dad as a chaperone on your first date. Fortunately for me, both the game and the home building project had groups of sailors signed up to support, so I decided to just engraft myself within each group to be inconspicuous.

We were told the drive down to the Orange Bowl was about thirty miles or forty-five minutes in good traffic. We were provided with a fifteen-passenger minivan to get us down there. Half of the van's sailors were going to the football game and the other half were going to a Miami Heat basketball game. It was decided that the football game would be the first stop and then the van would double-back to the basketball game. We were dropped off in a neighborhood near the Orange Bowl as to not get stuck in the traffic leading to the stadium parking lots. As we walked, I marveled at all the cars parked on the front lawns of people's homes. It seems that the homeowners were charging fans twenty to fifty dollars per vehicle for the convenience of not having to battle for a space in the stadium parking lots. It was the same all the way to the stadium: block after block, front yards filled with cars. *Man, this team has quite a fan-base*, I thought.

The atmosphere inside the stadium was electric. I could feel that the Miami fans were ready for this game. The Hurricanes held the number three ranking in the nation and the mood the fans created inside was primed for an upset. I saw many poster signs mocking the Hokie mascot—some funny, some distasteful. This was definitely a hyper-partisan crowd save one of our brave young officers, Ensign Rhett Breeden. Mr. Breeden was a Virginia Tech grad and he proudly wore his Hokie sweatshirt to the game. *Not going to be sitting next to him*, I thought.

Our seats were in a nosebleed section above the corner of the end zone, which was not surprising since the tickets were free, compliments of our sponsors. As fate would have it, Ensign Breeden's seat was right next to mine. *Maybe he will realize we are in "enemy territory." Maybe he will keep a low profile. Maybe he will keep his cheering down a bit and blend in with the crowd.*

"And here comes the Virginia Tech Hokies," the announcer said.

"Go Tech! Go Hokies! Woohoo! Yeah!" yelled Mr. Breeden.

And maybe it will snow in Cuba.

"Boo!" came the rousing crescendo from the crowd that lasted well past the last player coming onto the field. Their noise completely drowned out the cheers from Mr. Breeden.

The game was quickly becoming a rout: Miami was up fourteen to zero in the first quarter. Each time they scored, a thunderous deafening cheer came from the crowd, which was something I expected. Each time they scored, the fans hurled whole oranges into the end zone from every level of the stadium, which was something I never expected. *Crazy!* These oranges caused a delay-of-game penalty against the Hurricanes, which was assessed on the following kick-off.

Virginia Tech's quarterback was a favorite for the Heisman Trophy that season. He was playing with an injured ankle and did not receive any sympathy from the crowd.

CLAP-CLAP CLAP, CLAP, CLAP—"O-VER RA—TED!"

CLAP-CLAP CLAP, CLAP, CLAP—"O-VER RA—TED!"

CLAP-CLAP CLAP, CLAP, CLAP—"O-VER RA—TED!"

"Oh! I can feel the love, Mr. Breeden," I said trying to shout over the thunderous chant of the crowd.

"C'mon Chaps! It is just the first half," he said.

"Mr. Breeden, Tech is going to lose! Can't you see?"

"HE'S TO THE TEN...THE FIVE...TOUCHDOWN, HURRICANES!" shouted the announcer as a running back sprinted past the goal line.

Miami scored, the crowd roared, and more oranges were in the end zone. It just seemed to be the way things were going to go for the Hokies that day. To their credit, Virginia Tech put up twenty-one points on the board by game's end, but still lost by twenty points.

No luck with finding a Liberty Buddy. It was a good policy, though, for sailors and for life in general.

HABITAT FOR HUMANITY
Hope and promise fulfilled

05 November 2000

The next morning, I mustered on the pier with the group heading to the home building project. We took a short ride across town to a quiet suburban area that had modest middle class homes. As we pulled up to the building site, several workers inside and outside the structure were engaged in their work. The site looked like it had been cleared from an overgrown, abandoned lot. The concrete slab construction, ranch style home had vinyl siding but no roof.

Our point-of-contact (POC) stepped away from his work to greet us at the van. Even though he worked for a non-profit organization, he looked like a professional contractor: hefty, un-shaven, worn T-shirt, jeans, construction boots, and a sagging utility belt filled with tools. He split our group among several different tasks. I was assigned to work on the roof, which I thought would be interesting.

"Do you know how to use a nail gun?" he asked.

"No, but I understand the concept," I said.

I took a few practice shots on a spare piece of wood to improve my accuracy. Then I mounted the ladder and climbed to the roof.

There was a team of people putting in the beams. I had the assignment of securing the plywood boards that would become the foundation for the roof. The work was slow and deliberate: *measure twice, cut once*. I had to keep in mind that we were not building a tree house but *somebody's* house, built to last a lifetime or longer.

The other "roofers" introduced themselves as I made it to the top of the house. Several were volunteers from Coral Ridge Presbyterian Church. I told them I was familiar with their pastor through their television ministry. As we talked, I discerned that I was the rookie as far as home-building projects were concerned. They had been volunteering with Habitat for Humanity for several years and had helped build many homes in the Fort Lauderdale area.

I thought I was getting pretty good with securing the plywood to the beams of the roof. That is, until I received some correction from the site POC.

"Hey, watch your nail spacing. You are punching them into the plywood too far apart," he told me.

"Here, watch," he said, punching in a few nails for an example to follow.

"Okay. Thanks. I think I've got it," I said.

"What do you do for your ship?" he asked.

"I am the chaplain."

"You are the Chaplain? That is a good deal!" he exclaimed.

"How long have you worked construction?" I asked.

"About two years," he told me.

"Wow! You seem like you have done this for decades," I said.

"I used to work as a high-priced defense lawyer out in Hollywood. 'Making six-figures,'" he said.

"How did you end up here, in Florida, working for Habitat?"

"Living 'Life in the Fast Lane.' Drugs and alcohol took me down to rock bottom. I lost it all. Then someone shared about salvation in Christ. Now, I do this for a living. I help give people a new life. Just like somebody did for me," he explained.

His answer silenced me. I was a bit convicted because I never pegged this guy for a Christian.

"Chaps, don't judge a book..."

Forgive me, Lord.

Later in the day, a car pulled up and a woman stepped out. Our POC tapped me on the shoulder and said, "That is her, Chaplain. She is the one with whom we building the home".

"Looking good! Looking *real* good!" the woman exclaimed with a sense of pride.

All the volunteers stopped their work for a moment to happily greet her and show her the progress they made. She marveled at how well it was going and she seemed eager to "roll up her sleeves" to join in.

The overwhelming thought I had been this: Now I get it. A Habitat house was hope and promise fulfilled—all in one! A new life, just like the POC said.

-8-

WORSHIP SERVICE AT SEA

The sea always wins

12 November 2000
Early Morning

I awoke to the ship pitching, dipping, and swaying; it made me lose my balance when I got out of bed. It was Sunday and my first worship service at sea. I needed to get prepared. I managed to shower and make it back to my stateroom without stumbling. When I opened the hatch, there were several books, papers, and pens strewn on the deck, which had fallen because they were not secured. I felt that I needed to go topside, to see what the seas were like and perhaps get a forecast for the rest of the day.

Once dressed, I headed for the Wardroom for breakfast. I took about two bites of my waffles and noticed my appetite was gone. I tried to finish my juice but a quick sip was all that I could manage. Queasiness had started to affect my stomach. I took a deep breath, which made it temporarily dissipate. Then, I turned in my plate and silverware to the scullery and headed toward the Pilot House.

I reached the Pilot House and looked out the windows: overcast rainy skies, heavy seas with wind-whipped whitecaps, and the bow of the ship dipping and rising within them. All the sailors on the Watch seemed to be doing okay, standing with legs spread-eagle to help maintain their balance. I saw the Navigator standing by the Chart Table so I decided to go ask him about the forecast.

When he saw me coming his way, he said, "What do you have going on at 0900?"

"Protestant Worship," I replied.

"Hmmm," he muttered sarcastically as he peered forward through the windows.

"Don't worry, NAV. It is going to work out," I assured him.

I told myself, *God has got this.*

The queasiness returned and I headed back to my stateroom to sit down for a bit before service began. I was taking more and more deep breaths as I made my way down the ladder but now even that was not working to settle my stomach. When I reached my room, all I could think about was lying down on my couch. I shut my eyes, continued the deep breaths for several minutes, and to my surprise, the queasiness was ceasing. I remained in that position for about ten minutes and then the sick feeling was gone. I could sit up and even stand with no problem. What a remedy!

I made my way down to the Mess Deck and crossed over to the First Class Petty Officer's Mess, staggering all the way. RP1 Bates was there and he had the chairs and altar vestments set up and ready to go.

"How are you doing, Sir?" he asked.

"I am okay. Hanging in there," I said.

"Pretty 'hairy' out here today," he said. "Are you okay to do service?"

"Yeah, I am good right now."

"Is everything set up correctly? I put the communion hosts on the plate to the left and the challis with grape juice is there as well."

"Everything looks fine," I said.

"I hung your robe and stole over there."

"Okay. What time do people usually show up?" I asked.

"Let's see. If it is 0845, they will start showing up in about five to ten minutes."

People started to file in just as RP1 said they would. I was surprised to see the XO in attendance. He sat in the front row with six other sailors.

"Anything else, Sir?" RP1 asked.

"No. I think we are all set."

The ship was still rocking and swaying around and so was my stomach. I went back to my deep breathing to keep it settled. It was working somewhat and then another huge swell came, which almost made those seated slide across the deck.

Stay focused. You can do this. It was time to begin.

"Good Morning! Welcome to the nine o'clock Protestant Service. I am Chaplain Brown, your new chaplain. I am pleased to be here for my first worship service at sea. Please take your bulletins and stand. We will begin with the Doxology. It is printed in your bulletin."

My stomach was sour.

Hold it together
(deep breath)
Hold it together
(deep breath)

Looking at the sailors, I said, "Let's repeat the Doxology together."

(deep breath)

The congregation recited, "Praise God from whom all blessings flow. Praise Him all creatures here below. Praise Him above, Ye heavenly hosts. Praise Father, Son, and Holy Ghost. Amen."

Next, I was *supposed* to read, "I was glad when they said to me, 'Let us go into the house of the Lord.'"

However, what I *actually* said was, "Garbage can!"

(deep breath)

The congregation did a double-take in the bulletin, a bit confused by what I just said.

"Garbage can," I said again.

There! Out of the corner of my eye, to my right, against the bulkhead at the front row of seats—there it was! I dropped my bulletin and bolted over toward it just in time for the first heave of vomit to leave my mouth. Most of it made it into the can. I was doubled over, my gut in a knot, and unable to breathe for a moment. My abdominal muscles relaxed and I began to take deep and rapid breaths, which became shortened in anticipation of the second heave. Everything made it into the can this time. There were third and fourth dry heaves, which were mainly gooey saliva.

By this time, I had a small crowd around me to provide assistance. Closest were the XO and RP1 Bates. I overhead them ask for napkins from the Mess Deck and a mop and bucket from the storeroom. I caught my breath long enough to say to the congregation, "Service is over. I am sorry."

The XO ordered RP1 to escort me back up to my stateroom. I felt so miserable. I welcomed his assistance.

"Lay down, Sir, and take it easy," he said.

"I am sorry, RP1, I am so sorry."

"No need to apologize, Sir. It happens to the best of us," he said. "Just lie down and relax. It ought to help you feel better."

"I am sorry," I said again, now lying on my back.

"Sir, no need to apologize. Just relax. It *really* happens to the best of us. I will check on you later," he said as he turned off the light and shut the door.

Why, God? Why did you let this happen? My first worship at sea, why?

Noon

The nap did me well. I thought I would get up, grab a quick bite to eat, and relax a bit more. No sooner had I come to a sitting position, my stomach became uneasy. I lay back down, frustrated that I could not shake this sickening feeling.

Why, God? WHY!?

Mid-Afternoon

No change. In fact, the ship was intermittently hitting huge swells that rose so high it made me feel lighter. Then it dipped so steeply I felt like my spine was going to be pulled through the bed cushion. There was no fighting it. I just had to ride it out.

The longer I lay there the more my anger at God increased. *Why would He put me out there like that? This was my very first worship service. I am going to become a big joke around the ship!*

Why, God? WHY!?

Early Evening

The dinner hours had come and gone and I didn't care. Though the seas had somewhat settled, my stomach and attitude had not. All I could think about was how I failed and how everyone was going to see me now. *New Chaps can't hack it.*

From my prone position, I began to scan the room through the darkness. I could not see much but listened to the frame of the room creak and squeal with the swaying of the ship. *This was an old ship, thirty-years-old to be exact. Do the math: one chaplain about every two years, fourteen to fifteen predecessors, who have been here in this room. They have done what I am doing, probably have been through worse. For thirty years they had to tough it out and care for the crew. I am not the first or the last to deal with this.*

I mustered enough strength to find a seat at my desk, spending the next half hour in prayer asking God to forgive me for my poor attitude and complaints. Regardless of how I felt, I had a responsibility to continue to serve. The evening prayer was just a few hours away and I had nothing to say.

Gracious Lord, grant me the words that you want me to reach the crew with this evening. I release my talents, gifts, and abilities to you that they may be used to your glory, in Jesus' name, Amen.

Pilot House
2145

No one on the Watch mentioned this morning's incident or asked how I was feeling. It was like nothing ever happened. I was thankful for the silence. I just wanted to focus on giving the prayer then head back to my room.

"Ready, Chaps?" asked the Boatswain Mate.

"Yes."

"TATTOO, TATTOO! LIGHTS OUT IN FIVE MINUTES! STAND BY FOR THE EVENING PRAYER!"

Humility before the Sea

Let us pray.

Since the dawn of time, men have stood on shore, peered out over the waters, and wondered, What is out there? Perhaps when our apprehension gave way to curiosity, we began to set sail: vessels made of thatched papyrus reeds, gutted tree trunks, and stretched animal skins. The more we fared, we began to discover some basic laws:
"RED SUN IN THE MORNING..."
"RED SUN AT NIGHT..."
Long before the pharaohs reclined in stately craft on the Nile or the Inuit trekked across the icy arctic depths.
Before the Phoenicians' skill became legend or Alexander the Great spread Hellenism into Asia.
Before Carthage engaged Rome or Leif Ericson came aground in Newfoundland.
Before Columbus spotted Santo Domingo or Vespucci began to map the East Coast.
Before Americans replaced the Wooden Hull with the Ironclad and eventually the Steel Dreadnought.
Lord, you set in order statues that govern the wind, water, and sky. Seafarers across the ages have come to respect and abide by them—and we are not

exempt! For we own the sea as much as one can own the warmth of the sun.
Its vastness delivers to us a sober perspective each time we put out from the
shore. We are but mere tenants that are allowed to traverse
its breadth and depth.
Sovereign God, we acknowledge that you are Lord over the wind, water, and
sky. We look to you to harness these elements in our favor
whenever we journey upon the waters.
In your Mighty Name we pray,
Amen.

"TAPS, TAPS, LIGHTS OUT! ALL HANDS TURN TO YOUR BUNKS.
MAINTAIN SILENCE ABOUT THE DECKS. TAPS!"

The next day I got up, swallowed my pride, and was prepared to be the brunt of jokes in the Wardroom and about the ship. To my surprise, the exact opposite happened. I received many, "You doing okay, Chaps?" Shipmates who had been standoffish were now stopping to talking to me. It was obvious that everybody knew what happened but they did not seem to care. It was like my seasick episode was a rite of passage, almost as if I was a "Sailor" now. It was the strangest icebreaker I have ever experienced.

How could God take an incident in which I failed so miserably
and use it to establish relationships with the crew?

NAVAL WEAPONS STATION YORKTOWN

Meeting "Bish"

14 November 2000

The Ammunition Offload was the next evolution for the ship. We were nearing the end of our underway period coming into port just a few hours' journey from home at the Naval Weapons Station in Yorktown. However, this was no time to be complacent. Even though we felt confident—we had been underway for over two weeks—meticulous attention to all safety guidelines and precautions had to be followed once we arrived and began transferring ammunition.

The transit up to the Naval Weapons Station in Yorktown was a deliberately slow and careful evolution: exit Chesapeake Bay and enter the York River, pass Hampton, Poquoson, and Newport News, go under the Coleman Bridge at Gloucester Point, and moor at the weapons station. Our port briefs to the officers and chiefs emphasized the serious nature of offload operations. The Weapons Officer, Combat Cargo Officer, and Safety Officer all stressed the same message:

Safety was paramount, no rush to finish, and no cutting corners!

The captain would only grant on-base Liberty after the days' work was completed.

Liberty was sounded in the early evening and all sailors had to walk to the end of the pier to catch the shuttle buses to the main side of the base. It was a cool, overcast late autumn evening, which was in stark contrast to the welcoming warmth of Fort Lauderdale. I reached the first bus and found it packed with only one open seat left. I took the seat next to a Sailor that must have recognized me. His body language revealed he was not enthused to have me sit next to him. His shipmates seated behind us preyed upon his awkwardness.

"Sit up straight, Bish," one Sailor said.

"Say 'Please' and 'Thank You,' Bish" chimed in another.

"Hey, knock it off," he responded.

The giggles and snarky comments continued for a moment. The Sailor was staring out the window, which was fogged over with condensation. I broke the silence between us by introducing myself.

"Hey. I am Chaplain Brown," I said extending my hand.

"Hello, Sir. IT2 Bishundat," he replied with a handshake.

"Whom do you work for?" I asked.

"Operations Department. LT Coleman is my Division Officer," he said.

"The COMMO? I've heard he is quite the character."

"Yes, Sir. He is," he said.

"Where are you from?" I asked.

"A small town in Maryland, called Waldorf. You have probably never heard of it."

"Actually, I know all about Waldorf," I said.

"You do?"

"Yep! It is off of Route 301, by Saint Charles and La Plata," I said.

"No way! How did you know that?" he asked sounding surprised.

"I have driven through Waldorf for years, since I was a kid. Route 301 was our family's shortcut down to Richmond. We would often stop off in Waldorf on the way."

"That is crazy. Nobody has heard of Waldorf," he said.

"Well, I have," I told him.

We continued to talk as the bus made its way down the road through the dense woods in the secure area of the base over to the main side of the base. He shared about his girlfriend back home—about their plans for the future—and even showed me a picture of her that he had in his wallet. He was a bright and articulate young Sailor but he also had dashing good looks topped off with a million-watt smile that made him look like a movie star. It was clear that this guy was going places.

The Recreation Center had all the morale boosting basics: arcade games, pool tables, fast food menu, soft drinks, beer, and a smoking area outside the building. I sat alone and settled in on a juicy cheeseburger, fries, and a coke. Although we did not have off-base Liberty, this break from the ship was good and many sailors took advantage of it. I was the "early bird," deciding to head back to the ship shortly after I finished dinner. I left the young sailors to stay behind and close the place down.

Back to Sea
17 November

With our work complete at Yorktown, we headed back out to sea for a few more days to conduct navigation and steering checks and flight operations. In total, we had spent over two and one-half weeks underway excluding Liberty ports. I learned some important lessons:

Freedom is not free.
A Liberty buddy is hard to find.
The Orange Bowl has avid and rabid football fans. (Whew!)
COMRELs (Community Relation projects) are a
rewarding way of serving others.
*When it comes to my physiology vs. the sea, the sea **always** wins.*

-10-

STANDOWN
Be careful for what you ask

January 2001

The ship enjoyed a long break in the underway schedule by remaining in port from mid-December through the end of January. This permitted the crew to take Leave either in Norfolk or out of the area. Our family decided to stay put. This was our first Christmas and New Year in our new home.

The daily in port schedule began with Officer's Call. The XO led his meeting in the Wardroom Lounge each morning at 0630. He used it to review the plan-of-the-day and as a forum for the rest of the officers to pass information. On this occasion, the captain attended because he wanted to brief us on an important matter affecting the crew. He was concerned with the growing pattern of misconduct among newly joined, first-term sailors and wanted to poll the Wardroom for ideas on how to correct it. When he requested solutions, the officers began to vent.

"Sir, you cannot change how eighteen to twenty-year-olds act."

"Sir, kids these days are over-privileged and self-centered."

"Sir, they do not want to work hard and follow the rules. They think they can get over."

"Sir, some kids are just going to mess up. There is nothing we can do about it."

I was stewing on the inside. I knew we could make a difference in these young sailors but I did not speak up because I felt I was in the vast minority. The captain halted the comments as they were all beginning to sound the same. He left the Wardroom with the same concern:

Too many new-joins are getting in trouble and we need to find a way to fix it.

When I got back to my stateroom, I fired off an email to the captain:
From: CHAPS@SHREVEPORT
To: CO@SHREVEPORT
Subject: Sailor Misconduct

Sir,
With due respect to my fellow officers, I know that we can make a difference in these young sailors' lives. We can keep them on the "straight and narrow" and keep them in the Navy as well. I have a program that I think will be able to accomplish this and I would like the opportunity to try it.

Very respectfully,
Chaplain Brown

From: CO@SHREVEPORT
To: CHAPS@SHREVEPORT
Re: Sailor Misconduct

Chaplain,
Make it so!
R,
CO

"Make it so" from the captain, meant, "make it happen—now!" This was an instance where my heart got out in front of my head. The program existed in theory and not on a spreadsheet. The only experience I had with something similar was back at Great Lakes when I worked with sailors who were already in trouble—on Restriction or in the Brig—and the captain was looking for something proactive and preventive. It did not even have a name!

Okay, think! Who is the target audience? New sailors. And what are we trying to get them to do? Better behavior. How? We want them to adjust to shipboard life. New sailors to adjust, acclimate, and assimilate. We want new sailors to assimilate to the culture of shipboard life. New Sailor Assimilation...New Sailor Assimilation Course—that's it! Can it be an acronym? NSAC—yes! Perfect! That's it! NSAC."

With a name for the program, I now had to build the framework. That would come later and by that time I could fully pitch the program to the XO, officers, and chief petty officers. I could not do this alone. I had to brief RP1 Bates and seek his advice on how to get started.

Okay, Chaps, you have got some work to do, I thought. I had stepped out in faith and God provided an opportunity that was bigger than my desire.

-11-

WORK-UPS

The Deployment starts here

February 2001

Every ship in the Navy has what is known as a Work-Up Cycle. It normally entails months of arduous training at sea prior to the standard and regularly scheduled overseas deployment. Whether it is a Carrier Battle Group (BATGRU), Destroyer Squadron (DESRON), or an Amphibious Ready Group (ARG), work-ups were the way to certify that ships and their sailors were ready to deploy.

Our first evolution was the Type Commander's Amphibious Training or TCAT. It was a weeklong exercise that involved the three ships of our ARG— BATAAN, SHREVEPORT, and WHIDBEY ISLAND—as well as Marines from various units at Camp Lejeune, North Carolina. TCAT allowed both sailors and Marines to work closely together during very basic amphibious evolutions such as ship-to-shore movements—in the air from the Flight Deck and on the sea from the Well Deck. It also provided the opportunity for the ARG to sharpen their ship-handling skills as well as conduct training drills that were integral to the performance of each ship. TCAT was just the tip of a training iceberg that was seven months deep.

02 February
Transit to Onslow Bay, North Carolina

Our ship had just ventured past the Virginia Capes Operating Area (VACAPES) when the Captain came over the 1MC:

"Onboard Shreveport, this is the Captain. Let me have your attention. One of our sister ships has just reported a man overboard. They have requested any vessels in the area to assist with the search for their shipmate. We are going to halt our transit to Onslow Bay and stay in VACAPES to help them. I encourage as many of you who are able, to go outside the skin of the ship—to the Flight Deck, Weather Decks—and lend your eyes to the search for our shipmate. That is all."

TCAT had to be delayed because our mission now was to prowl the area in search of a missing Sailor. I began to pray privately for his quick recovery because the waters were very cold this time of year—not higher than 50 degrees—and the evening was approaching fast. I felt for the captain on the ship of the missing Sailor. He is ultimately responsible for every soul onboard his vessel. I thought of the family of that Sailor who would be on the receiving end of this difficult news.

When I reached the Flight Deck, there were other sailors lined on its perimeter scanning the surface of the waters. There were aircraft high overhead—Coast Guard and Navy—assisting with the search. By dusk, there was still no sign of the Sailor and those of us who were on the Flight Deck had left to go back inside away from the cold air and encroaching darkness.

If we did not find this Sailor *soon, our efforts would turn from a Search and Rescue mission to a Search and Recovery.*

02 February

The next morning word about the ship was we had been released from assisting in the search for the Sailor. Everybody knew what that meant but the captain made it official through an announcement over the 1MC. He told us that the recovery efforts would continue but we were released around midnight to head south for Onslow Bay. I made a mental note to include a group prayer during tomorrow's Protestant Worship Service. However, the Lord led me to catch the crew's attention, just for a moment, about this Sailor during the evening prayer.

One Life

Let us pray.

Tonight we ponder the importance of one life.

Numerous ships, aircraft, and personnel were tasked with searching for...one life.

We gave our best efforts to locate and recover...one life.
We altered schedules, training plans, and our course in the hope of finding...one life... lost at sea.

We would do it all over again, especially for one our shipmates. The investment of time and energy cannot compare to what it is worth.

O Lord, one life—each life—is of profound worth and value to you.
You surround us with your love because we mean so very much to you.
The sky, the stars, and the heavens should be a bit jealous of the attention you pay to one life. Even the ones who love us cannot rival the affection you bestow on one life.

Thank you, Lord, for deeming one life—our lives—
as having infinite importance in your sight.

Amen.

03 February

Onslow Bay, North Carolina

"FLIGHT QUARTERS, FLIGHT QUARTERS! ALL HANDS MAN YOUR FLIGHT QUARTERS STATIONS! WEAR NO COVERS TOPSIDE. THROW NO ARTICLES OVER THE SIDE. ALL HANDS NOT INVOLVED WITH FLIGHT QUARTERS STAND CLEAR OF THE FLIGHT DECK, HANGAR BAY, AND WEATHER DECKS!"

The announcement over the 1MC began our day shortly after breakfast. It was the signal that we would be receiving and sending helicopters (HELOS) to and from our ship. CH-46 HELOS would be ferrying Marines and conducting Deck Landing Qualifications throughout the day. Marines would also be arriving on the sea's surface via Amphibious Assault Vehicles (AAVs) launched from the shore. They would enter the back of the ship through the Well Deck, which was ballasted down to allow seawater to partially fill it so that the AAVs could operate inside the ship.

I was anxious to see Marines again. The three years I spent serving with them in Twentynine Palms, California gave me an appreciation for their unique culture and it also taught me to "speak their language." Even though it would be easy to meet and mingle with them once they came aboard, I had to resist that temptation and remain "Blue" (serving the Navy) because now I was a shipboard chaplain and not a "Green" (serving Marines) chaplain.

Mid-Afternoon

My computer was really acting up. The monitor turned strange colors and the processing time between webpages was as quick as cold molasses. When I could not put up with it any longer, I asked RP1 Bates for advice.

"Sir, we need to call the ITs to come and take a look at it," he told me.

"Make the call, RP1," I said.

It was frustrating! Everything I did aboard ship was predicated on my computer working properly. With a poor computer, there was no communication inside the ship or to the outside world; administration came to a halt and ministry was hindered.

RP1 hung up the phone and told me that the IT Shop was sending help in about ten to fifteen minutes. A knock came about that time and RP1 opened the hatch.

"Petty Officer Bishundat, come on in!" said RP1.

"Hey RP1. Do you have computer problems?" asked Bish.

"Yes. Come on in IT2. It is the chaplain's computer," he said.

"Bish! Am I glad to see you!" I said with relief. "I am about to throw this machine overboard!"

"No need to do that, Sir," Bish said with a slight chuckle. "What seems to be the problem?"

"Here, take a look. The screen has turned all these strange colors and the processing time from webpage to webpage is super slow. Can you help?"

"Let me see," he said taking a look at the screen. "It looks like your screen needs Degaussing."

"De-what-ing?" I asked.

"Degaussing. It is a pretty common occurrence with Cathode Ray Tube monitors."

"I'm sorry, Bish. Cathode Ray Tube?"

"Yes, Sir. CRT monitors, like your television at home. You see, Degaussing is necessary when the magnetic field that is emitted by CRT monitors..."

I was with him for about the first thirty seconds and then I got lost in the deep trail of his intelligence. When he finished, I think I understood about 10 percent of his total explanation.

"Okay, that is great, Bish. Can you fix it?" I asked.

"Oh sure, Sir! That is no problem. However, I am afraid that you are stuck with the CPU's speed of processing. I cannot fix that until we get back to Norfolk," he said.

"You mean I just have to put up with it?" I asked.

"Yes, Sir. If I had another one in our inventory I would bring it to you," he said.

"Okay, well I will get out of your way and let you work on the screen. Thanks again for your help, Bish."

"No problem, Sir," he said.

"RP1, I am heading out to do some deckplate ministry among the sailors and Marines. I will catch up with you later," I said.

"Okay, Sir. I will see you later," said RP1.

I grabbed my cover and headed out of the office, shutting the hatch behind me.

Man, that's a smart kid!

"THE SHIP IS AT FLIGHT QUARTERS. ALL HANDS NOT INVOLVED WITH FLIGHT QUARTERS STAND CLEAR OF THE FLIGHT DECK, HANGAR BAY, AND WEATHER DECKS!"

I could not help it but as the chaplain, my ears were very sensitive to the amount of profanity that I heard about the decks of the ship. There is a cliché that says, "You cuss like Sailor!" I understood what it meant but I disagreed with its premise. Having served first with Marines and now with sailors, I can honestly say that, regarding profanity, sailors and Marines were tied with each other. Neither service had a corner on this behavior trait nor would trying to curb it have made any difference. *That* would have been like handing out speeding tickets at the Daytona 500.

While sailors and Marines have traditionally had a love-hate relationship, their mission is so inextricably linked that one would think no contentiousness would ever exist between them. But it does—a fondness and friction that normally centers on this: which is the better Service? I have overheard sailors remind the Marines of the words that appear on their emblem: "Department *of* the Navy...United States Marine Corps", the inference being Marines were merely a subordinate component of the Navy. This would prompt Marines to respond, "Yes, we are a 'Department of the Navy'—the *men's* department!" Inferring that Marines are always the testosterone-tough component of the sea services.

Which one was truly the better Service? It depends on whom you ask. However, regarding the use of profanity—in my opinion—sailors and Marines were tied. They are equal. They are the same.

2155
Pilot House

Rest

Let us pray.

There are many who pray: "Give us more blessings, O Lord.
Look on us with kindness!"
But the joy that you have given me is more than they will ever have
with all their grain and wine.
When I lie down, I go to sleep in peace; you alone,
O Lord, keep me perfectly safe.[2]

Find rest, once again, O weary one.
Find rest in God, our Savior.

Gracious Lord, this evening rest is a hidden treasure
that we so desperately need to find.
Enrich and replenish us with the peace you provide while we sleep.
Even if it is just a few hours here and there before we relieve the
Watch, use it, somehow, to restore our strength. For today's work has
exhausted us. We are far from missions' end and from home.
In you alone we find peaceful rest.
Then we recline with confidence, safely surrounded by your presence.

Find rest, once again, O weary one.
Find rest, in God our Savior.

Amen.

---

[2] Psalm 4:6-8

"TAPS, TAPS, LIGHTS OUT! ALL HANDS TURN TO YOUR BUNKS. MAINTAIN SILENCE ABOUT THE DECKS. TAPS!"

05 February
"SET CONDITION 1-ALPHA FOR WELL DECK OPERATIONS! SET CONDITION 1-ALPHA FOR WELL DECK OPERATIONS!"

The AAVs would be joining the ships today making their transit to us a couple miles offshore. I was curious to see how they operated at sea. They were quite conspicuous and noisy on land.

My experience with AAVs and their crews was out in Twentynine Palms, California with Delta Company, 3rd AAV Battalion. We called them "Delta Tracks." They roamed the desert in support of the numerous training and combined arms exercises. Even though I was serving with the infantry, I had grown fond of "trackers," primarily because they were the ones that ferried Marines from my battalion to their training objectives. They traveled in serials of five to seven vehicles, so I got a lot of ministry accomplished at one time when they parked for the evening.

From the starboard side Bridge Wing, I could see the AAVs as they approached our ship from a distance. To my surprise, they seemed to be silenced by the noise of the ship, flight operations, and the muffle of the sea. One-by-one, they "swam" over the lowered Stern Gate and into the Well Deck of the ship. Their arrival meant more Marines were coming aboard, which normally translated into more crowded passageways, longer chow lines on the Mess Deck, and a bigger crowd in the Wardroom.

I made it a deliberate practice to enter the Wardroom through its front hatch. Most of the officers used the short cut entrances from the Wardroom Lounge or galley. It was a quicker and more convenient way to get to chow. That did not matter to me. What mattered was paying homage to the countless African-American sailors who were denied the access and privilege of becoming a naval officer, thus, becoming part of the Wardroom. For much of the Navy's history, many African-American sailors could only: serve officers their meals, clean the tables, wash the dishes, scour pots and pans, and swab the deck. So from day one of my commissioning as an officer, I told myself that if I ever served aboard a ship, this would be my practice: always enter through the font hatch, use the proper etiquette when requesting a seat at the table, sit down, and dine for all who desired but were denied this opportunity.

As I expected, the Wardroom was crowded with officers—both Navy and Marine—so finding an open seat for lunch was a bit of a challenge. I was about grab a plate and utensils when I noticed a familiar face among the Marines. It was Chaplain Rob Askiew, a colleague of mine from the AME Church. I quickly put down my plate, got out of line, and headed over to the table where he sat. He rose from his seat as his eyes caught me moving towards him.

"Rob! Man, you are a sight for sore eyes! I said. "What are you doing out here?" We extended hands, shook them, and ended the greeting with a brief hug.

"Hey Brother, it is great to see you!" he said. "You are the last person I expected to see out here."

"Same here," I said smiling in agreement. "When did you get here?"

"I came aboard this morning on one of the AAVs. My Marines are doing some amphibious training this week so I hopped on one of the tracks to join them," he said.

"I know! That is why we are down here, too," I said. "What a blessing it is to see you!"

"Grab a plate and come sit down," he said.

"Sure, I will be back in a moment. Don't go anywhere!" I said.

Chaplain Askiew was from our Eleventh Episcopal District, which is the entire state of Florida. He had been on active duty for just about as long as I had. We talked for a while, sharing "sea stories," the latest news from our church, and about our families. I learned that he was only going to be aboard ship for the day then head back to shore in an AAV in the early evening.

How special it was to meet up with a fellow AME Chaplain at sea! There were so few of us serving in the Navy to begin with and to actually train and serve alongside one was a rare treat.

"TATTOO, TATTOO! LIGHTS OUT IN FIVE MINUTES! STAND BY FOR THE EVENING PRAYER."

God's Nature

Let us pray.
O God, tonight we ponder the essence of your nature and the expression of
your character.

Peace
The sweet, calm assurance of your presence that transcends the turbulence of
any situation and it is available upon request.

Love
The boundless force of affection aimed directly at us. It embraces us in spite of
our own self-esteem, yet, seeks no return receipt.

Compassion
You understand our hopes, needs, and fears.
You remember how we are made.
You care for us until the end.

Grace
We do not deserve your unmerited favor.
Why do you show it?
It is ours and it is free.

Mercy
We are spared the penalty of our actions.
The verdict is in: not guilty, time and time again.

Forgiveness
If you kept a record of our faults, who could stand before you?
We get a brand new start, multiple chances to make things right.

Truth
It is the only language you speak.
The only currency you spend.
The only path you travel.

Holy
Do we really understand what it is to be completely clean
inside and out?
Everything we touch is left smudged with the ink of human nature.
But your impression, O God, is beyond immaculate.

TCAT continues, the operational tempo seems relentless,
and the hazards of our work still remain.
Our petition of you is simple:

Surround us.
Protect us.
Restore us.
Be with us.

Amen.

06 February

We had a break and a special guest today. The captain had been invited to meet with the Amphibious Squadron (PHIBRON) Commander over on the USS BATAAN. This created an impromptu pause in the exercise. In exchange, Chaplain Hogan, a Roman Catholic priest, would pay us a visit from the BATAAN on the "Holy HELO," as it is known when a chaplain is aboard the helicopter. We expected the Captain to be gone for most of the day.

"FLIGHT QUARTERS, FLIGHT QUARTERS! ALL HANDS MAN YOUR FLIGHT QUARTERS STATIONS! WEAR NO COVERS TOPSIDE. THROW NO ARTICLES OVER THE SIDE. ALL HANDS NOT INVOLVED WITH FLIGHT QUARTERS STAND CLEAR OF THE FLIGHT DECK, HANGAR BAY, AND WEATHER DECKS!"

It was my job to meet Chaplain Hogan in the Hangar Bay when he arrived. I asked RP1 Bates to be there as well to give him a proper greeting. When we arrived, the captain was already there with other Navy and Marine officers preparing for the arrival of the helicopter. He wore goggles, an aircraft cranial with ear protection, and a float coat over his uniform.

"Good morning, Sir!" I said greeting him.

"Good morning, Chaplain," he replied.

"Heading over for the meeting, Sir?"

"Yeah. Say a prayer. I am not big on flying," he said.

"Yes Sir! No worries. You will be fine," I said.

"GREEN DECK!" came the announcement from the 5MC—the Flight Ops Control intercom—signaling that the first helicopter's arrival was imminent. The Aviation Boatswains Mates (ABs) were in place on the Flight Deck and their attention was focused on the sky, specifically in the direction of the helicopter. Now, everyone in the hangar could hear the encroaching noise of its rotors. The ABs were in position with the primary in a yellow jersey directing the landing. As the helicopter hovered directly over his head, he raised his arms and hands to provide the pilot with the typical landing signals that would align the aircraft with a designated spot on the Flight Deck. The AB continued his final landing signals, bracing his legs in place against the deck to resist the heavy downdraft caused by the helicopter's rotors. It was now at ten feet, five feet...safe landing on deck!

Several ABs with blue jerseys ran out under the helicopter and applied wheel chocks to the tires and chains with hooks on each end to secure the aircraft to the ship. With the helicopter secure, passengers debarked from the rear and walked across the Flight Deck into the Hangar Bay. I spotted Chaplain Hogan and walked over to great him.

"Hey, Sir! Welcome Aboard!" I said elevating my voice because of the helicopter noise.

"Thanks Chaplain Brown. It was a quick flight," he said. "RP1, how are you?"

"Fine, Sir!" responded RP1.

"Sir, let's get you inside so you can drop off your things. You are just in time for lunch. Would you like to join me, Sir?" I asked.

"Sure! That would be great," he said.

As I was escorting Chaplain Hogan up to the Wardroom, I heard over the 1MC four bells and this announcement:

"*SHREVEPORT, DEPARTING!*"

This meant that the helicopter carrying the captain was departing the ship. One last bell signaled that he had left the ship.

The captain spent most of the day on the BATAAN meeting with the PHIBRON Commander, which allowed Chaplain Hogan plenty of time to conduct ministry. His presence turned a Tuesday afternoon into an "Instant Sunday." He celebrated a Mass, took confessions, and provided mentoring to our Roman Catholic Lay Leader.

Breather

Let us pray.

Thank you God for the much needed break in the training schedule. It was a welcome pause, a moment to catch our breath, and exhale.

Laughter came to relieve the tense vigilance inherent to training. Our hearts are bursting with thanksgiving!

Thanks for sun kissed skies and calm seas; they reflect your glory in Creation.

Thanks for travel mercies for our Captain and the Marine Officers from the SHREVEPORT to the BATAAN and back.
Thanks for the "Holy HELO" ride that brought Father Hogan aboard.
Thanks for the ministry he provided and the new acquaintances he made.
Thanks for working parties of sailors and Marines: cleaning, painting, waxing decks, and buffing brass from bow-to-stern, above and below, and around the ship.
Thanks for safe Air Ops.
Thanks for medical care for an injured Marine.

Thanks for a moment to exhale; it prepares us to draw new breath, new life, and new strength for a new day built upon the unexpected.
Thank you, Lord, for the pause, for the break, for the laughter, for the moment—just a moment—to catch our breath and exhale.

Amen.

07 February
"REVEILLE, REVEILLE! ALL HANDS HEAVE OUT! BREAKFAST FOR THE CREW!"

I was going into "The Pit" today: the Forward Main Machinery Room (MMR), or engine room, as it is commonly known. There were actually two MMRs—Forward and Aft—but RP1 recommended that we visit the Forward Space, as it is where Main Control was located. He arranged for one of his colleagues from the First Class Petty Officer's Mess to meet us and provide a tour of the space.

This was my first venture into the world of the Machinist Mate and I had heard two things about it: it was at the bottom of ship and it was hot. However, I believed that I was up for the challenge. After serving for several years in the baking heat of the Mojave Desert sun, I felt pretty confident that I could call on that conditioning to prepare me for this experience.

RP1 Bates led the way, taking me to a Modified Zebra hatch that had only a round scuttle opening that went down below to the next deck. He went through the scuttle first with no problems. I kneeled down and put one leg through the scuttle until my foot rested on the ladder leading down to the next deck. I noticed that the opening seemed pretty narrow before I placed myself in it and I was right. There was only two or three inches clearance around my waist. With both feet firmly planted on the ladder, I slipped through the scuttle and began to descend the ladder into the next deck passageway.

"Phew! Anymore of those Mod Zebra scuttles, RP1?" I asked.

"No, Sir. Just ladder wells all the way to down to the pit," he said.

"I can feel the temperature difference already. It is starting to get a little warm," I noticed.

"Oh, you have not felt warm yet, Sir. Just wait," he said.

Several more decks passed and the further we went down the more the temperature rose. We stopped at the end of the final ladder, which was the entrance hatch to the Forward MMR.

"Okay, Sir. Before we go in, we have to put on our hearing protection," he said raising his voice above the elevated noise on the other side.

"Alright. I have them," I said, pulling out two Styrofoam earplugs. I placed them in my ears and gave RP1 the thumbs up signaling that I was ready to go inside.

"Here we go," said RP1 as he pulled up the lever on the watertight door. A rush of stifling hot and humid air met us as the door opened. The temperature inside must have been ten to fifteen degrees higher than outside. I saw sailors at work scattered throughout the space and thought, *Sauna! These guys work in a sauna!*

We met up with RP1's colleague who was on Watch and he provided us with a walking tour of the space. He stopped to point out several pieces of equipment and a watch station. He spoke with a loud voice so he could be heard over the boisterous grinding, pounding, pumping, and rotating of all the gears and machinery.

I started to sweat.

At first I kept ahead of it by wiping off my face and brow. Then it spread, covering my head, dripping down my neck, and making a moist mess of my undershirt. I scaled the wiping down to just my eyes when I realized that I could not get ahead of it.

The sailors I met on my tour did not talk much to me or to each other. After brief but cordial greetings, they went back to manning their stations, monitoring gauges, or cleaning and maintaining machinery. I could not figure out if it was the noise, the heat, or something else that kept conversation down to a minimum. However, I knew I was disoriented and uncomfortable down here. I was ready to leave. Then it hit me. *If there are men down here, then there is ministry to be had, but how? How could I cope down here, let alone reach anyone with the message of God's love?*

Lord, show me the ministry here in the midst of the heat, noise, sweat, and silence of this place.

08 February
TCAT ENDEX (End of Exercise)

I used this day of transit back to Norfolk to continue ministry of presence about the ship. I found the best ministry took place late at night from midnight until 0300 in the most obscure places: the Signal Bridge at the top of the ship, Aft Lookout at the stern, and Shaft Alley at the very bottom. The sailors I met at these spots seemed to really appreciate a visit from the chaplain.

Through TCAT, God was allowing me to "learn the ship," expanding the scope of ministry and deepening my bond with the crew.

-12-

ANTIGUA
Caribbean Cruising

15 March 2001

What the ship missed by in being in port for January, she made up during the month of February. Three separate underway periods, each no more than a week long, were spread out over the entire month. They were normal operations trips for an amphibious vessel, which meant brief pauses in transit at Lynnhaven Inlet to pick up a Landing Craft Unit (LCU) from the Naval Amphibious Base in Little Creek and ship-to-shore embarkations of aircraft and assault vehicles in Onslow Bay, North Carolina. These evolutions were great for me personally because it allowed me to learn the ship, her crew, and grow my sea legs just a little longer.

Here is what else I discovered:

An Amphibious Transport Dock (LPD) had a crew of eight departments that could be categorized into three distinct groups according to common professional characteristics. They were Air/Medical/Dental/Supply, Operations/Navigation, and Deck/Engineering. I arranged these groups according to how I learned to approach each with pastoral care.

The AIR group was the most congenial and "chaplain-friendly" of the three. My presence was welcome in their workspaces without having to prepare much in advance. *Dare I call them "regular folk"?* To inquire how I could support them I simply asked, "Hey Shipmate, how can I help you?"

The OPERATIONS group basically asked, "What do you want?" when the chaplain was in their proximity. This community deals with handling and transmitting sensitive information ranging from SECRET to CLASSIFIED so they can be very tight lipped, reserving trust for only those they work with closely. They were high-functioning individuals who were very smart, clever, and did not miss a thing. A chaplain who spent too much time in their space without a clear purpose may be considered suspect.

The DECK Group inquired, "How long can you hang?" In order to "hang" with these sailors, I had to be willing to engage them in their arduous dust, grease-and-grime filled evolutions, and workspaces. They handled the heavy equipment such as the ship's anchors, boat and aircraft crane, fire-fighting tools, line handling, and stood Watch in the engine rooms. They are the "blue collar breed," the tough guys, "meat-and-potato" sailors who physically give 110 percent every day. For instance, the ship's engine rooms' average temperatures are about 98 degrees with the same relative humidity. Those who are unaccustomed to that environment usually visit and leave within fifteen minutes. Thus, sweat is the calling card of all steam engineers. So their specific query of the chaplain was "How long can you hang, and sweat, with me?" A chaplain who could not "hang" and spent too little time with them would seem superficial and irrelevant.

And then there were the Marines, who were an entity all their own. Ronald Reagan once said, "Some people go their whole life wondering if they ever made a difference. Marines don't have that problem." What images and thoughts go through your mind when you hear the title, "United States Marines?" Exactly! These guys were the substance of legend, whose prowess in battle spoke for itself. Marines are confident can-do kind of people who invite rather than ask the chaplain, "Come and go with me." Marines wanted me to be with them and do what they do but not as they do. There is a fine line: in appearance, physical training, and forced marches, in the desert, in the jungle, or "any clime and place." Be with them but *be* the chaplain, specifically, be *their* chaplain. A chaplain who was not interested in doing what they did was pretty much a dead duck in their estimation.

Why the effort to grasp such diversity? The crew and embarked personnel—1400 souls strong—needed to be reached with God's love and I had to be able to speak their language in order to do so. This basic ministry-at-sea principle reflects the words of Paul, the apostle, "So I become all things to all men, so that I may save some of them by whatever means are possible" (1 Corinthians 9:22). I considered the challenge before me both privilege and pleasure.

The underway periods in February also allowed me to meet other Christian members of the crew, primarily through the worship services. There were three men with whom I felt strong connections: First Lieutenant Kevin Adams, the Electronic Maintenance Officer Ensign Derby Luckie, and Ship's Serviceman Chief Gregory Ducass. I had both First Lieutenant Adams and Ensign Luckie pegged as my Liberty buddies, because they were married men-of-faith, and Chief Ducass as my partner-in-prayer. Chief and I met just about every morning in my stateroom for prayer and we were mutually great sources of encouragement for each other. These meetings eventually branched out to become the Daily Prayer Meeting, a gathering of Christians each day at 1230 in the Strategic Arms Coordination Center or SACC.

We were heading to Antigua, an island nation in the West Indies, in the Leeward Islands of the Caribbean. Our primary mission was to conduct the Final Evaluation Problem, or FEP. This qualification operation gauged the ship's ability to conduct multiple combat missions and support functions simultaneously with casualty control situations, while demonstrating the capability to deploy. On our way down to Antigua, the crew would practice such exercises over several days. We would then pick up our evaluators in Puerto Rico and conduct the actual evaluation on the way back to Norfolk.

I was curious to see if Antigua was home to any AME churches. I thought it would be a great idea to visit while on Liberty. All the islands of the Caribbean were located in the Sixteenth Episcopal District of our church. So I decided to contact the bishop who presided over that district in order to get a definitive answer, which he promptly provided:

From: BISHOP@16THAMEC
To: CHAPS@SHREVEPORT
Re: Antigua Visit

Chaplain Brown,
I am sorry to say that we do not have any churches in the area you mentioned. Please keep trying. I would love to have you fellowship with our folks.

In Christ,
Bishop DeVeaux

From: CHAPS@SHREVEPORT
To: BISHOP@16THAMEC
Re: Antigua Visit

Bishop DeVeaux,
Thanks for all your efforts! Since I am on such a mobile platform, I just thought that I would give it a try to connect with our fellow AMEs on the island. When our ship heads to New York later this spring, I will make the same effort to connect with local congregations there too.

Thanks again and may the Lord bless you and yours!

Sincerely,
Chaplain David Brown

26 March
Underway for Antigua
From: CHAPS@SHREVEPORT
To: RB@HOME

Subject: Some Foul Weather

Hey!

We have just run into some rainy weather as we continue to head south— nothing too serious, though. It sort of reminds me of those rain showers we encountered in Puerto Rico where part of the sky was cloudy but you could look to another part and the sun was shining bright. We have also crossed over into the Atlantic Time Zone, which means we had to move our clocks ahead one hour last night.

Tomorrow I begin my first run of my New Sailor Assimilation Course (NSAC) at 0830 in the Chief Petty Officer's Mess. I have about eighteen sailors signed up and I am in the process of nailing down the last few details. The captain signed off on an official 5050 Notice, which sort of makes the program "law" around here. I have had nothing but positive feedback and support from my colleagues. Please pray for the Lord's blessing upon it and that it will help us keep the sailors we receive.

I am going to forward some emails to you from our command point of contact for Antigua, Chief Ducass. The chief is of Jamaican descent and speaks with a heavy accent but he has proven to be a reliable source of information on the island. He is also a believer and is on fire for the Lord.

I will write more soon (very soon).

Take care,
Chaps

Chief Ducass, sought to provide as much information about Antigua to the entire crew as possible in multiple email messages throughout the day. I think he accomplished that mission:

From: SHC DUCASS@SHREVEPORT
To: ALL SHREVEPORT
Subject: Antigua Tips

0658

Good morning Ladies and Gentlemen!

Antigua is a former British colony, gaining total independence in 1982, so there is still a residue of the British there. For example, tea is a very popular hot drink. There is strictness with manners; "Good morning", "Good afternoon", and "Good night" are entrenched courtesies. The water is perfectly safe and potable. The Rastafarians, are a religious group of people, they are thousands of them on the Island, although they may appear intimidating, they are friendly. They mostly keep to themselves, do not consume salt and do not believe in birth control. An obvious cultural difference that you will find is, West Indians in general are an affable set of people. They hug a lot and may be extremely close to you while speaking. This is just their friendly nature.

Thanks Ladies and Gentlemen,
Chief.

0841

Good morning Ladies and Gentlemen!

I have a few more brief Antigua tips for you. The beaches start out quite shallow, but get suddenly deep. Be cautious of sea urchins residing in the reef. The market in Saint John's is a must see, displaying a tropical array of fruits; mangoes, coconuts, guavas, sugar cane, and pomegranates. They are all fairly inexpensive. All shopping for souvenirs should be accomplished at Heritage Park. It is duty free and less pricey. If you shop at some of the private vendors their price may be more, in anticipation of the ship's arrival. For all the non-alcoholic drinkers, the internationally award-winning Ting Grapefruit Drink is widely available. It is both tasty and nutritious.

Thanks Ladies and Gentlemen,
Chief

0918
Good morning Ladies and Gentlemen,
I was of the genuine opinion I was disseminating sufficient information
to you about this island paradise. However, in excess of twenty sailors just
stopped me in the passageway and asked the same questions. Sugar cane
although scientifically classified as a form of grass, is considered to be a
fruit. Throughout the West Indies it is extremely popular and sugar is a main
earner of foreign exchange. Sugar cane is similar in appearance to bamboo,
but it has a semi-hard light yellow matting in the inside and a greenish strip
of skin externally. It is widely available, normally very sweet, and extremely
good for minting clean teeth. You can go native and use your teeth to peel
the skin off or have the vendor peel it for you with a knife or machete. Please
be careful when using your teeth to peel the skin. You may see some residents
and many Rastafarians displaying the colors, red, green, black, and gold. Red
is for the blood of the people, gold is for the sunshine, black is for the people
(since Antigua is 70 percent black), and green is for the vegetation. You will
probably see watchbands, hats, shirts, and belts reflecting these colors.

Thanks Ladies and Gentlemen,
Chief.

1137
Good morning Ladies and Gentlemen,
A few brief points on Antigua. Generally Antigua is a Christian-minded
country. Their culture, heritage, and the way of life are different from life
in the US. Some of the profane and lewd words often used in the Navy,
would be considered an insult towards them. Antigua/Barbuda maintain
an average temperature of between 85 to 90 degrees daily, however, the
Island is kept fairly cool by the trade winds, which routinely blow through
the entire West Indies region.

Thanks Ladies and Gentlemen,
V/r Chief.

1421

Good afternoon Ladies and Gentlemen,
A few quick points of interest: Antigua has a socialist democratic political system. They have two major political parties, with five-year terms. The political climate is different from the States. Politics is a passionate subject and not routinely discussed. Instead of Senators, they have ministers: Minister of Security, Minister of Agriculture, and Minister of Local Government. The Prime Minister of Antigua/Barbuda, is the equivalent of a president.

Thanks Ladies and Gentlemen.

1842

Good evening Ladies and Gentlemen,
The US dollar is widely accepted. I strongly suggest you utilize it, but ensure you receive the correct change in EC dollars. For you coffee drinkers, the number one rated coffee in the world, Blue Mountain Coffee is available. It can be acquired in the Tidewater Area, but it is extremely expensive. Visa, MasterCard, and American Express credit cards are widely accepted. In most ports you would hear, "Be careful of pick pockets," but not here. Honesty is one of their trademarks. Cock fighting is acceptable and there is limited casino gambling in the larger hotels.

Thanks Ladies and Gentlemen,
Chief.

1913

Good evening Ladies and Gentlemen,
I have been asked what local foods in Antigua I recommend and their cost. The following culinary delights are well known West Indian dishes: curry goat, curry chicken, jerk chicken, jerk pork, oxtail and butter beans, stew

peas and rice, shrimp and *escovitch* fish. *Escovitch* fish, is fish in onion, vinegar, eskellion (scallion), thyme, pimento seeds, and West Indian Scotch Bonnet pepper. When you are finished eating, you can wash it down with passion drink, coconut water (not coconut milk) or a cold Red Stripe beer. The total meal costs a measly eight to ten American dollars. Take it from me: it is finger licking good!

Thanks Ladies and Gentlemen,
V/r, Chief.

From: CHAPS@SHREVEPORT
To: RB@HOME
Re: Some Foul Weather

Hey!

The rain has passed and we are under a brilliant dome of sunshine. We are also at General Quarters right now so we cannot go outside and enjoy it. Sort of ironic, huh? As I mentioned earlier, we will be finished with our practice training today. Tomorrow will be one big field day, which means cleaning the entire ship. The captain is going to stop the ship about 100 miles from Antigua and do a "Swim Call" for any sailors who want to take an early dip in the warm waters of the Caribbean. I will be watching from the ship, thank you very much! We are too far from shore and there are too many sharks in the water.

More details to follow as we travel...

Take care,
Chaps

"TATTOO, TATTOO! LIGHTS OUT IN FIVE MINUTES! STAND BY FOR THE EVENING PRAYER."

Dependence

Gracious Lord, it is right and good that we should depend upon each other.
Dependence is an integral part of what makes us mission capable. Every day
we have to depend on the experience, training and skill of our shipmates.
Indeed, aboard SHREVEPORT there are not any unimportant people.

But there is something else we can depend on that does not always bid in our
favor—the unpredictable nature of life. Plans change often, circumstances
evolve, and situations are not always as they seem. People disappoint, though,
they do not intend to do so. Staying flexible sometimes offers little relief to
the stress that our training environment causes. Even our mistakes may be
unintentional or self-inflicted but are usually most telling
of our own fallibility.
We need something rock solid and secure, something quintessentially dependable.

What do we do and where can we go?
Who can we turn to for relief, strength, security, and peace?

O Lord, lift us from every fear that makes us self-conscious and suspicious.
Bring us up and out to a place where our faith and confidence in you abounds.
O Lord, lead us beyond frustration to a place of implicit trust in you that
brings peace and happiness to our lives.
O Lord, protect us from the hidden hazards that are inherent to our
profession. Build a hedge of safety around us that is lined with your presence
and reinforced by your power.
O Lord, love us in a way that we may not understand,
certainly do not deserve, but graciously receive.

Then, we shall discover that you are the solid foundation upon
which we can confidently construct our lives.

Amen.

27 March
From: CHAPS@SHREVEPORT
To: RB@HOME
Subject: Last day at sea

Hey!

Today was our last at sea so the captain decided to hold a Swim Call in the middle of the ocean. We stopped the ship and lowered the Stern Gate at the back of the ship into the water so that the sailors could walk off the ship and into the sea. It was sort of like walking the plank! Again, it is my opinion that this is the "sharks' domain" and we have no business doing recreational swimming out here. They did have a patrol boat, buoys, rescue swimmers, and sailors manning rifles from the Flight Deck. Still, I figured, if a shark was to come and attack you it would come up from below where you cannot see it. By the time you noticed, it would be too late. I did, however get some photos of those who took the plunge. It is amazing that even with calm seas, two to four foot waves made swimming and staying afloat a difficult task. After spending just ten minutes in the water, many sailors were exhausted and needed help to get back on the ship. I will get my chance to swim during our port visit.

The New Sailor Assimilation Course was a success! Every new Sailor that joined since February came to the course and they seemed interested in being there. RP1 Bates will continue to track their progress. My goal is to not lose any of the sailors that we get from Great Lakes. With the Lord's help, I truly believe we can do that.

By this time tomorrow, we should be moored at the pier in Saint Thomas, Antigua. I hope that being connected to direct current electricity and phone lines will allow us to communicate at regular speed through email. If not, we will have to stick to the six-hour thing, which requires a lot of patience. I will give you a phone call, though, as soon as my feet get on dry land.

Love you both!
Chaps

From: CHAPS@SHREVEPORT
To: RB@HOME
Subject: Somewhere beyond Puerto Rico

Hey!

We have just journeyed beyond Puerto Rico through what is called the Virgin Pass. It gets its name from the Virgin Islands and you actually do pass between Saint Thomas (Port) and Puerto Rico (Starboard). We had a clear day with unrestricted visibility so both islands were in view simultaneously. Tonight we are getting our last port briefs concerning culture and security. The command is doing everything possible to make sure that the crew is on its best behavior.

I miss you guys very much. I hope that it is a quiet and peaceful night for you both. Write back when you can.

Take care,
Chaps

As I prepared evening prayer, the Lord led me to address the matter of conduct while on Liberty in Antigua. It was a bit risky since I had never prayed before with such a preachy tone. However, I got past any lingering apprehensions by reminding myself that the evening prayer was still God's moment and not my own.
"TATTOO, TATTOO! LIGHTS OUT IN FIVE MINUTES! STAND BY FOR THE EVENING PRAYER."

Good Conduct

Gracious Lord, once again you have shown yourself to be completely faithful in providing for our needs. Thus far, we have enjoyed a smooth transit down to Antigua and you even thought enough of us to throw in a safe Swim Call for good measure. As our destination draws near, help us to consider the following:

Sensible people will see trouble coming and avoid it, but an unthinking person will walk right into it and regret it later. (Proverbs 22:3)

Lord, people do not trip over boulders; their own shoelaces usually will do. However, if you give us the opportunity to behold danger from afar, do not let foolishness or ignorance blind us from getting out of the way. Keep us from the error of poor decision-making and help us consider our ways and pursue a path that is pleasing to you. Let our decisions preserve and protect our lives and the lives of our shipmates.

If you have to choose between a good reputation and great wealth, choose a good reputation. (Proverbs 22:1)

Lord, we greet this island nation with our reputation fully intact. We have earned the right to be representatives of the greatest Navy and democracy on earth. We are so blessed that we sometimes do not realize that our principles and ideals are the envy of other nations. It would be a travesty to disregard that reputation for the sake of personal prerogatives. Keep our ship far from shame, our national identity distant from dishonor, and our families away from disgrace. A good reputation is worth far more than gold. Once it has been tarnished, there is no amount of wealth in the world that can restore it.

All of us should eat and drink and enjoy what we have worked for. It is the gift of God. (Ecclesiastes 3:13)

Lord, SHREVEPORT has proven her ability to not only work hard but to roll with the punches of a changing schedule, rebound from the frustrations of equipment failures, and cope with the sacrifice of leaving loved ones behind at home. Therefore, Liberty is deservedly a good thing! It gives us a moment to exhale and draw a deep breath of leisure and relaxation. Thank you for the gift of freedom to enjoy this port visit.

Lord, finally, please remind us that freedom is always tethered to a sense of responsibility. We should be content that we have earned the privilege to enjoy the island culture of Antigua but impress upon our hearts that having fun and doing the right thing are never mutually exclusive. Give us the resolve to leave Antigua a better place than we found it.

In your Holy Name,
Amen.

"TAPS, TAPS, LIGHTS OUT! ALL HANDS TURN TO YOUR BUNKS. MAINTAIN SILENCE ABOUT THE DECKS. TAPS!"

28 March
0852
From: RB@HOME
To: CHAPS@SHREVEPORT
Re: Somewhere beyond Puerto Rico

Hi Chaps!

By the time you get this, you should be in Antigua. Sounds like thing are going well so far. Things on the home front are fine except it is "Brrrrr" cold here! It was below freezing last night. Oh, if you could only send some of that nice tropical weather this way! They say it should warm up somewhat this week and the weekend should be pretty nice.

I am glad your NSAC Class went well. Sounds like a winner for the Navy. Thanks for taking the time to send those updates from Chief Ducass. They really give us something to look forward to during this time. Email when you can.

RB

"MOORED! SHIFT COLORS!"

We made it—Saint John's, Antigua! The whole crew wanted to get right off the ship but we had to be patient. No one was going to leave until we received the Liberty briefs and the captain put down Liberty Call. The officers and chiefs made their way into the Wardroom to get ready for the briefs. The Bull Ensign positioned himself at the front hatch waiting to call everyone to attention once the captain arrived with the briefing team.

"Stand By!" called out the Bull Ensign. We all stood up from our seats at each table.

"Attention-on-Deck!" barked out the Ensign.

"Carry on! Please be seated," said the Captain as he entered the room.

His entourage was comprised of local officials as well as two military attachés representing United States Southern Command (SOUTHCOM). The officers from SOUTHCOM were an Army Lieutenant Colonel and a US Coast Guard Lieutenant Junior Grade. The Army Lieutenant Colonel briefed on security matters, admonishing us all to be aware that we were representing our Nation in a foreign country while the Coast Guard Lieutenant Junior Grade was our liaison for a COMREL planned in Saint John's later in the evening. The local officials briefed on the "gouge" —good info—such as transportation to shops, hotels and beaches, local currency exchange, moped and bicycle rentals, and restaurants. Once the brief was done, I took a moment to speak with the Coast Guard officer to get some specifics regarding the COMREL project. She told me there would be a meeting to discuss possible projects but that was all the information she had. The meeting would take place at the local Red Cross office on the outskirts of town at 1900. Transportation would be provided. Afterwards, I went back to my stateroom to change into civilian clothes. I was just about done when the announcement came over the 1MC:

"LIBERTY CALL, LIBERTY CALL! LIBERTY CALL FOR DUTY SECTIONS ONE, THREE, FIVE, AND SEVEN. LIBERTY EXPIRES ON 30 MARCH AT 0700."

I knew that I had to find my prospective Liberty buddies—at least one—so that I could head out on the town. Both were still tied up with work in their divisions so the only choice I had was to hitch on with a group of officers who were going to do "safe" things and be back at the ship at a decent hour. I had to catch a ride out to the Community Relations Project in the morning.

About 1400

I noticed that we were docked on the more industrial side of the port. The seemingly more affable and affluent side was host to the large, white cruise ships and they catered to the tourists with long rows of duty-free shopping. No matter. We were just glad to be getting off the ship and into our first evening of Liberty. We were informed at the Liberty brief that it would be cheaper to take the local buses into Saint John's than to grab a taxi. The group of officers that I was with heeded that advice and took the bus ride, which was cheap—only two Eastern Caribbean dollars. Each one of us had to sit where we could, separate from our buddies, and find a seat, as the bus was crowded with Antiguans.

It was a slightly warm and humid ride downtown as the air conditioning struggled to overcome the outside air temps and the collective body heat on the bus. I noticed most of the officers seated in the rows ahead of me keeping each other within eyeshot. At certain stops, I noticed the presence of poverty and it was unlike ours in America. I saw whole impoverished neighborhoods; their streets were filled with people who seemed neither despondent nor in despair. *Fascinating!*

The music on the bus was reggae all the way! I did not recognize much of it, but the songs had a mesmerizing affect. I found myself getting caught up in its relaxed and melodic syncopation and it put me in an "island-mood" for the rest of the trip. We were coming to our stop when a tune that I recognized caught my ears. *Ah! That is Bob Marley— "One Love"!* My head started to bob a bit to the rhythm but I did not want to be so conspicuous with its movement that another officer would notice. The lyrics were as familiar as a friend's firm handshake:

> *"One Love! One Heart!*
> *Let's get together and feel alright.*
> *Hear the children cryin' (One Love)*
> *Hear the children cryin' (One Heart)*
> *Give thanks and praise the Lord and we will feel alright*
> *Let's get together and feel alright."*

I departed the bus at our stop in Saint John's but that tune remained with me for the rest of the evening.

From: CHAPS@SHREVEPORT
To: RB@HOME
Subject: A great day in Antigua

Hey!

It was great to talk to you on the phone this evening. I already told you about the day that I had. The Antiguan people are as friendly and warm as Chief Ducass stated in his briefing notes. They are a jovial, at-ease people, close-talkers, very touchy-feely and if you did not know that beforehand, you would probably find them to be a bit overbearing.

Most of the crew is still off the ship and will probably stay in town overnight. The captain has extended a liberal Liberty policy saying you do not have to return to the ship if you do not have duty. That means people will be gone for two days after they stand duty. I have got a free bed here aboard ship so they can go right ahead and pay 150 to 200 dollars per night to live it up in town.

I miss you very much. I will try to send you some photos by email before we leave.

Love,
Chaps

From: CHAPS@SHREVEPORT
To: XO@SHREVEPORT
Subject: Red Cross meeting and church visit

Sir,

I attended the meeting at the Antigua and Barbuda Red Cross Headquarters this evening. Unfortunately, it seems that the only job they have now is a potential paint project that they were planning to begin well after we leave. However, they did mention that they had some material needs such as CPR Mannequins and Micro Shields they have been unable to purchase due to lack of funding. I am going to speak to Doc Buxton about this need and contact our local chapter of the American Red Cross once we return.

The church service that followed the Red Cross meeting was held at Central Baptist Church, which is situated high on a hilltop in downtown Saint John's. From the front of the church, the whole of Saint John's harbor is in view and I could easily see the ship moored starboard side to.

The people were warm and receptive and were expecting to see me. It seems that Lieutenant James—SOUTHCOM—who was at the in port brief this morning, contacted the pastor ahead of time. The service was actually a Bible study split by gender; the women met in the sanctuary while the men met outside on the front porch. Also, LTCOL Churchill —SOUTHCOM— was in the congregation and gave me a ride back to the ship.

All in all, it was a great evening.

Very respectfully,
Chaplain Brown

30 March
From: CHAPS@SHREVEPORT
To: RB@HOME

Subject: Another great day in Antigua

In a nutshell, today was a great day. As I mentioned, five other officers and I took a three-mile bicycle ride across the Antiguan countryside to a beautiful beach on the eastern side of the island. The trip proved beneficial for physical therapy and to take in the scenery. The area outside of Saint John's is rural farmland that is blooming with tropical flowers. Goats, horses, and cows roam about the roads freely. Do you remember when we used to ride through the Mojave National Preserve in Cima, California and we saw the cows we thought were free but were behind the fence? The animals here have no boundaries so you must keep your eyes peeled at all times.

When we arrived at the beach we were greeted by the typical vendors who wanted to sell everything from jewelry to Jet Ski rides. The best part was the clear, turquoise blue water, which was calm, warm, and inviting. I spent a total of about an hour in the water and the rest of the time lying in the sun. I got pretty dark today. Also, if you remember, in Puerto Rico all the radio stations played salsa music all of the time. In Antigua its reggae, reggae, reggae! You hear so much of it that you begin to get caught up in that laid back, island frame of mind.

The ride back to the ship took a little longer because Mr. Luckie took a spill on his bike. He is okay but we had to stop and turn around to find him. Once we returned, we showered, got dressed, and headed to this restaurant called "Lashings by the Sea". The Lashings part of its name is derived from the chopping action that is applied to harvesting stalks of sugar cane. The restaurant's location used to be a sugar cane plantation but that has been abandoned so the only thing out there is the restaurant.

When we arrived, there were about ten other SHREVEPORT sailors already there having a good time. We sat down and ordered dinner. To my surprise the prices were very reasonable. I had the Chicken *Carnivale*, which was out of this world. It is made of chicken stewed in a sweet mango curry sauce with chunks of pineapple, tomatoes, basil, and garlic. It was fantastic! Mr. Luckie had the Shrimp Creole. That was out of sight too. Just as we were finishing dinner, two vanloads of SHREVEPORT sailors showed up for dinner and drinks. Even the captain and XO were there. The captain sat and talked with us for over an hour and he was his typical down-to-earth-self wearing a T-shirt, shorts, and sandals. We are blessed to have him as our CO. Under him, the crew is really pulling together. We got back to the ship around ten and called it a day. Tomorrow is snorkeling day and I will let you know how that goes. I may need to use the ATM but not for much money. I will let you know how much.

Love you both very much! I will talk to you tomorrow.

Take care,
Chaps

"THE UNDERWAY CHECKOFF LIST IS POSTED ON THE QUARTERDECK!"

31 March
From: CHAPS@SHREVEPORT

To: RB@HOME

Subject: On our way to Puerto Rico

Hey! We are on our way to Puerto Rico this evening and we should arrive sometime in the afternoon. As we were pulling away from the pier, some Antiguans were there waving goodbye to us but not as many as there were to greet us.

It seems the tourism dollar dictates the flow of life around here. The only regret I have is that I was unable to locate and purchase their famed Blue Mountain Coffee. I remember very well how much I enjoyed the native blend I picked up from Puerto Rico a few years back. I was anxious to try another local blend but the stores only had what I could buy in the states. Anyway, the Eastern Caribbean dollar, or EC as it is known, has a great exchange rate: one US dollar equals 2.65 EC dollars. If you shopped wisely then you could get some pretty good bargains.

I hope you had a pretty good day. Write back when you can.
Chaps

Coming Together

Gracious Lord, as we bid "farewell" to Antigua,
we carry with us many memories of the people and places
we have encountered along the way.
It was refreshing to have had this new experience;
observing each other on Liberty in Antigua has allowed us to see ourselves in
a different light. We have proven numerous times that we can
work hard together and now we understand that we can apply the same
standard to our common recreation. In many ways being on Liberty has
fostered a deeper appreciation and respect for each other.
It added a new perspective about our shipmates:

dimensions of personalities, likes and dislikes, each individual strand interweaving to form a fabric of common identity.

The gel is thickening.
There is a sense that we are coming together as a crew.

When a crew comes together, you can see it in their handshake, hear it in their conversation, and just tell that they possess something special.

When a crew comes together, they thrive on problem solving, anticipate troubleshooting, and in general, make the "rubber hit the road."

When a crew comes together, their similarities are accentuated and their differences are de-emphasized. The things they have in common are far more pertinent to accomplishing missions and quality of life.

When a crew comes together, they can disagree without being disagreeable. While at times they may not see eye to eye, it is understood that there is little profit in poking them out just to prove who is right.
When a crew comes together, they are willing to sacrifice their personal comfort to reach out to a shipmate in need. They realize that the cost of not reaching out is far greater.

O Lord, due to our imperfection and the demands of shipboard life, we admit, perhaps even reluctantly, that though a crew can come together the real challenge is staying together. Hence, our needs and our pleas tonight are nothing short of your Omnipotent hands joining to cusp and carry us home.

This we pray in your Holy Name,
Amen.

"TAPS, TAPS, LIGHTS OUT! ALL HANDS TURN TO YOUR BUNKS. MAINTAIN SILENCE ABOUT THE DECKS. TAPS!"

-13-

NORTH FOR NORFOLK
Working our way back home

01 April 2001
From: CHAPS@SHREVEPORT
To: RB@HOME

Re: On our way to Puerto Rico

Well, today was a blessed day aboard ship! As I write, we are anchored about a mile from the Naval Station Roosevelt Roads in Puerto Rico—so close, yet so far. As we were pulling closer to the island, I noticed that there were large rain clouds hovering over the mountains. I immediately thought of two things: it rains just about every day in Puerto Rico and the national rainforest is called *El Yunque.* Anyway, we came to anchor and I recognized the pier, the hospital, and not much else on base. We anchored to pick up the evaluators from Afloat Training Group (ATG) in Norfolk, who will be traveling with us all the way back home.

It seems that getting underway yesterday made everyone forget that today would be Sunday. Take a look at today's schedule of events:

0830-1030: General Quarters

1030-1130: Freshwater Wash-down/Clean the ship
1130-1300: Lunch
1330: Sea and Anchor Detail
1500: Anchorage at Roosevelt Roads

Guess where I had to put worship service? That's right, we had services today at 1600. Fortunately, God blessed us through having services at that time. I had been praying the Prayer of Jabez all day, specifically the part which asks the Lord for "more territory". Instead of having the service inside, we held it at the back of the ship on the Flight Deck in plain view of everyone. We had loudspeakers and microphones hooked up and we turned up the volume so that the whole ship could hear the service. God had bigger plans than that. Not only did the worship participants and the crew listen, but also sailors in the small boat providing security for our ship began to slow down and circle the ship. About four sailboats who heard our singing, praying, and preaching slowed down to listen too. That is not all! By the end of the service, rain clouds began to form and come our way. However, they stopped and went in a different direction, leaving a sunshine gap on the Flight Deck for us to complete worship. After the service was over, the captain came down to see how things went and I told him we had about ten people who showed up.

He was encouraged by the report and asked, "Did you see the rainbow?"
"What rainbow? I asked.
"There was a rainbow at the front of the ship while you were conducting services."
I wanted to shout right there on the spot! I went back to the Wardroom for dinner and sat down next to one of the officers who asked, "How is your day going?"

Well, I just had to brag about what the Lord had done. Moral of the story: It does not matter what we do. God is going to get His glory!

My heart and mind are set on Friday when we are scheduled to pull in late in the afternoon. We will be underway tomorrow morning heading for home.

Love you both!
Chaps

"TATTOO, TATTOO! LIGHTS OUT IN FIVE MINUTES! STAND BY FOR THE EVENING PRAYER."

Great Praise

Praise the Lord!
Let everything that has breath praise the Lord!

Gracious Lord, from one anchorage in Antigua to the one here in Puerto Rico
and to the one we look forward to the most—Norfolk—
we give you great praise.

For providing a space today on the Flight Deck for worship,
we give you great praise.
For the safe arrival of our guests from ATG, we give you great praise.

For a consistently calm sea state, we give you great praise.
For the "breather" in Antigua, we give you great praise.

For those who are this day one year older and one year wiser,
we give you great praise.
For all the unseen and unsung heroes aboard SHREVEPORT,
we give you great praise.

For the strength you provide to stand the "Mid" and
"Seven-to-Forever" watches,
we give you great praise.

For a crew that never quits, never bows out,
and consistently rise to the challenge,
we give you great praise.

For the care and protection you have provided for our loved ones,
we give you great praise.
For silent prayers that no one else hears, we give you great praise.

For being there when no one else understands, we give you great praise.
For the private struggle you help us overcome, we give you great praise.

For the mercy you show us when we fall, we give you great praise.
For the helping hand you offer us to get back up, we give you great praise.

For greeting us this morning, carrying us through the day,
and being by our side tonight, we give you great praise.
For the courage to ask for tomorrow's blessings this evening, we give you
great praise.

For the cohesive bond between shipmates, the skill, wisdom, and hustle to
execute the FEP, the opportunity to prove our mettle, and another chance to
come out on top, Lord, we give you great praise!

Praise the Lord!
Let everything that has breath praise the Lord!

Amen.

02 April
"REVEILLE, REVEILLE! ALL HANDS HEAVE OUT! BREAKFAST
FOR THE CREW!"
From: CHAPS@SHREVEPORT
To: RB@HOME

Subject: Offline for a few hours

Hey!

I am going to be out of contact for a few hours today. We are beginning our FEP and the evaluators are going to throw several scheduled training scenarios all at once. The main ones that will keep me busy are General Quarters (GQ) and the Mass Casualty Drill. Once GQ is sounded, I will have to run up three decks to get my gas mask. You are probably wondering why I do not have it on me in the first place. Well, the whole idea is to approach the scenario as if it were a surprise.

My place during GQ is in the medical spaces. I am there to provide pastoral care for the wounded and dying. I am not sure if the evaluators will rate the level of care I provide or not, but I will follow through on the training as if it were the real thing.

Write back when you can.
Love,
Chaps

One Day Closer

Let us pray.

"This is the day that the Lord has made. Let us rejoice and be glad in it."
(Psalm 118:24)

Sovereign God, we find ourselves steaming north one day closer to home yet just another day at sea.

One day closer to shooting a bearing off of Cheslight, rounding the corner at Cape Henry, and making that final turn at the Three Sisters.

Just another day at sea, arising at dawn: making musters and meetings and briefs, training, always training towards the goals and standards set before us.

One day closer to a car that has not turned over in two weeks, to the promise of a ride back to Pier 22, to a familiar voice received offshore for those blessed with cell phones.

Just another day at sea, filled with sweat and salt, heat and humidity, our intentions, motion and movements all at the direction of the ship's bell and the whistle of the Boatswain's pipe.
One day closer to a smile, a hug, or perhaps a kiss that has canvassed our daydreams and resided alongside our evening prayers.

Just another day at sea, depending upon and being there for each other without asking or seeking a return favor because that is just what shipmates do.

One day closer, yet, just another day at sea.

Or was it?

Did we really stop to consider the origin of this day?
Did someone check the sky last night to make sure that the Big Dipper was still facing Polaris? Did someone see Orion dip diagonally below the mountains?

Yes, we arose and all hands heaved out but who made the sun break over the horizon? We cannot count how many times we had to wipe the sweat from our foreheads but who was responsible for bathing us in such brilliant warmth?

Lord, we already have tomorrow down on paper. It is a file attached to our email or it has been buried in secret message traffic, as if we could completely know and control and understand the next twenty-four hours.

Lord God, tomorrow is your domain and you have already scanned its length and breadth. Humble our hearts, and let us stand in awe of you. We seek your face, your will guiding us to the precious gift of the new day before us. "This is the day that the Lord has made. We should rejoice and be glad in it."
(Psalm 118:24)

Amen.

"TAPS, TAPS, LIGHTS OUT! ALL HANDS TURN TO YOUR BUNKS. MAINTAIN SILENCE ABOUT THE DECKS. TAPS!"

03 April
From: RB@HOME
To: CHAPS@SHREVEPORT
Re: Offline for a few hours

Hey Chaps!

I know that you are busy with GQ. Just wanted to touch base to let you know the Christian Recorder came today. The first article was regarding the Martin Luther King, Jr. celebration at the Naval Station in Roosevelt Roads. Bishop DeVeaux was the guest speaker. The article quoted Chaplain Maurice Buford from the Naval Station Hospital. He said, "The AME Church should do more to encourage Itinerant Elders to consider ministry in the vineyards of the Armed Services." Another plus for the chaplains!

I hope all is going well aboard the ship. Let me know how your day went when you get the chance.

Love,
RB

From: CHAPS@SHREVEPORT
To: RB@HOME
Re: Offline for a few hours

Hey!

I am back! Whew! What a difference a few hours and a few hundred miles makes. I will explain: GQ ended about 1000 and then the seas started to get heavy. Although it was crystal clear with warm temperatures, the winds and the waves picked up out of nowhere. That usually means "run for the sea sick pills," which I did. They helped. But after lunch, we ran a Mass Casualty drill and that is when things became interesting. The seas climbed to eight to twelve feet almost immediately and anything not tied down went crashing, smashing, and spilling all over the place. The galley was the worst: grape jelly, honey, salt, pepper, spices, eggs—you name it! Even my office had printers and the copying machine tipped over on their sides. Of course, I went back upstairs and got "horizontal" after we finished the drill. It was all that my stomach could handle. I am debating whether or not to eat something because that episode has killed my appetite.

I am glad to see that Chaplain Buford had that article published in the Recorder. It was really shrewd of him to invite Bishop DeVeaux. He is an excellent speaker and practically guarantees front-page coverage in the newspaper. Uh-Oh! The seas are still pretty rough and my stomach is rumbling a bit. We are still in the Caribbean Sea and not heading home very fast because we have one more day of evaluations. Once we are done we will be heading home at top speed—about 20 knots.

I have attached a copy of last night's prayer to this message. The Holy Spirit working through a worn down chaplain, who just wanted to be home with his family, inspired it.

Love,
Chaps

Surprise Occurrence—"Grace under Fire"

Let us pray.

Gracious Lord, something happened today during the Mass Casualty drill that was noteworthy. As the drill was called away, the Medical Training Team sprang into action and the stretcher-bearers made their transit from the Flight Deck to the Mess Deck. The seas began to build right on cue as if it were some pre-planned variable from ATG to evaluate our reaction.

The duration and intensity of these waves were enough to soil the ship's galley with a deck-plate collage of sugar, tomatoes, mayonnaise, brownies, and broken glass. The waves were strong enough to topple triage tables and send sailors staggering to and fro. However, we made it through. We endured the test without incurring any actual casualties.

If we look closer there is a lesson here.

Lord, you never promised that things in life would be easy,
only that you would be with us.
You never promised that things in life would go our way,
only that you would make a way for us.
You never promised that we would understand the "why now?" and "why me?" situations of life. However, you promised you would provide everything we needed to endure them.

In life, fast runners do not always win the race, intelligent people do not always become wealthy, and the strong do not always survive. Endurance is the victor in the end.

Lord, you have blessed SHREVEPORT with the elastic quality that absorbs and rebounds, anticipates and reacts, and follows through to the finish line. We can endure because you are with us. You are a way-maker and you have equipped us for success. Please bless us even more so that during the FEP, just as in life, we will continually come out on top.
This we pray in your Mighty Name,
Amen.

04 April
From: CHAPS@SHREVEPORT
To: RB@HOME

Good morning!

Today we are doing some Underway Replenishment drills with the USS BATAAN. We will be pulling closely alongside her—about 200 yards away—and tying up lines to attach to each other while moving about twelve knots. It is a delicate operation requiring the full attention of the crew. Mr. Luckie is going to be the Conning Officer, or ship driver, because he has the Captain's trust and does this operation better than anyone else. Speaking of Mr. Luckie, he asked me if he could catch a ride down to Pier 22 on Friday, if that is okay.

Give our son a hug and kiss for me today and continue to pray.

Love Ya!
Chaps

From: CHAPS@SHREVEPORT
To: RB@HOME

I am having a good day and things are relatively quiet now. We are having a Steel Beach Picnic on the Flight Deck tomorrow. I volunteered to cook burgers and dogs along with four other sailors. All should go well provided that the weather and seas cooperate.

I am giving the chaplain's page on the ship's website a makeover. I am updating the Intro/Bio section from my predecessor and posting the evening prayer on a daily basis. This is part of the CO's initiative to keep the website current. It also provides a platform to expand ministry for the Lord.

The plans for Friday have not changed: Pier 3 at 1600. If there is any change I will email and let you know. Have a great evening!

Love,
Chaps

Anxious Anticipation

Let us pray.

O God, you are my God, and I long for you.
My whole being desires you; like a dry, worn out, and waterless land,
my soul is thirsty for you. (Psalm 63:1)

Oh, God of Peace, what should we do with a day so filled with anxious anticipation? We tried to stay busy but our minds became cluttered and distracted. There is still a job to do which requires we keep our head in the game. Perhaps some anxiety is useful because it can keep us on our toes lest we become careless and overlook the hazards inherent to shipboard life. However, we look to you tonight wishing we could push the "fast forward" button on the training tape deck and get back to Norfolk ASAP. Unfortunately, that is not possible.

And so we wait, rest, rise, relieve, muster, meet, plan, and train to sharpen our skill for battle and strengthen our resolve to fight.

We would like to escape this feeling of anxious anticipation but that is exactly the way you would like us to relate to you. You want us to get hungry, get thirsty, even a little desperate for you. Then, we would understand that waiting periods produce a dependence upon your strength and not our own. Then, we would experience a peace that is able to carry us through life's circumstantial deserts to the sweet, supernatural oasis of your tender loving care. Best of all, we could get to know you. We could sit down at your banquet

102

table of blessings and have a finger-licking, lip-smacking, spiritual soul-food feast. Nothing would be withheld!

O God, you are my God and I long for you. My whole being desires you; like a dry, worn out, and waterless land, my soul is thirsty for you.

Amen.

05 April
From: CHAPS@SHREVEPORT
To: RB@HOME
Subject: Good morning!

What a brilliant, clear, windy, and wavy morning we are having out sea. The sunrise was especially red-orange and beautiful. The old maritime saying goes, "Red Sun in the morning, sailors take warning." That usually means bad weather is looming on the horizon. But there is no way you would figure that with these crystal clear skies.

Things are going very well and the credit, praise, and glory goes to God! I have found that the crew is really tuning into the evening prayer. Usually there is some quiet chatter in the Pilot House just before the prayer. The Boatswain Mate—the man who pipes the whistle, rings the bell, and makes all announcements on the 1MC—will remind everyone on Watch to keep the noise level down. The Lord has it so that all I have to say is "Let us pray" and everyone gets quiet.

We have the Steel Beach Picnic planned for today. Oh! We passed our Final Evaluation Problem evolution—barely! The passing score was sixty-three and I think we scored a sixty-four so there is a lot of work to do between now and the deployment.

I am going topside to enjoy this beautiful morning.

You have a blessed day!
Love,
Chaps

Steel Beach Picnic

The Flight Deck was getting crowded with sailors anxiously waiting for the Steel Beach Picnic to begin. Much prep work went into the setup: two long rectangular charcoal grills, dual rows of tables for plates and utensils, bread rolls, sliced tomatoes, pickles and onions, baked beans, macaroni salad, relish and other condiments, and coolers filled with an assortment of canned soft drinks. The Mess Specialists had everything in place and ready to fire up the grill.

I was in charge of cooking the hamburgers and hot dogs for a couple of hours. Some were delighted, some were amused, and others were curious to see if I could pull it off. Nobody knew that in a former life I was a short-order cook and running a grill was no problem. I began with the burgers—two rows of eight patties—searing, flipping, and then stacking them on the cooler side of the grill. The dogs were lined at the top of the grill perpendicular to the grates. They cooked up rather quickly. Once one batch of meat was done, I was on the next.

"Chaplain, it looks like you have got some grilling skills," commented the captain as he fixed his plate.

"Yes, Sir. I was not always a chaplain," I responded.

I smelled of grilled charcoal smoke when I finished cooking. However, my first thought was not to take a shower. I was hungry so I filled a plate full of food and found a seat at the edge of the Flight Deck. I sighed and relaxed for a moment, immediately beginning to realize how tired my feet, ankles, and back were from standing so long.

Just for sport, the sailors converted the Helicopter Hangar into a mini boxing arena. They actually put together a ring with an elevated mat, ropes, poles, and boxing gloves for each contestant. The event was called, "The Boxing Smoker." I was not certain if the boxers were being paired by age or weight. It did not matter, though. The sailors in the audience enjoyed the fighting, cheering loudly at every wild punch that seemed to land squarely on the opposing boxer's face. There were no bets placed—that I could tell—and most fighters fared pretty well, only a few bloody noses and swollen eyes.

My attention to the action in the ring was drawn back to the Flight Deck when I noticed a Sailor chasing another Sailor with what looked to be a whipped cream pie in his hand. He caught up to the Sailor and threw the pie, slathering whipped cream across the back of his head and neck. *Strange,* I thought. *Was this a pie-eating contest gone badly?* I stepped out of the hangar and onto the Flight Deck. A few sailors had set up a pie station on the port side of the deck and for a while it seemed like they could not make up enough. The pie throwing quickly became random and indiscriminate; everyone was getting "creamed". The Flight Deck was awash with whipped cream spatter. The sailors were having a great time. It was hilarious to watch.

For a while, all the sailors were avoiding me and I hoped that would continue. Then, some began to notice that I was one of the few clean faces left. One Sailor got brave enough to approach me. I looked him in the eye and said, "You do it and you are going to Hell." He stopped, his smile dropped off his face, and he turned away. Even though I was joking, he was probably too superstitious to cross me.

Every time I said that, the sailors would pause, reconsider, and find another "victim."

Back in my stateroom, I finally relaxed for the evening. I was tired, smelled of smoke, and in a lighthearted mood. I suspected the crew was as well. We passed the FEP, no incidents on Liberty, and we were heading home. Life was good.

"TATTOO, TATTOO! LIGHTS OUT IN FIVE MINUTES! STAND BY FOR THE EVENING PRAYER."

Homecoming Rhyme

Gracious Lord,

About two weeks ago
yes, it was on a Friday,
SHREVEPORT pulled in her lines,
and got underway.

Steaming for the Caribbean
was the navigation plan,
to Antigua for Liberty,
for warmth, clear waters,
and perhaps get a tan.

But along the transit
we had much work to do,
cleaning ladder backs, angle irons,
and running to GQ.

"Prepare for the FEP!"
was heard the battle cry.
We trained every scenario,
so that nothing would go awry.

Far ahead of schedule,
though many hadn't noticed at all,
we stopped the ship in the sharks' domain,
and conducted a Swim Call.

We pulled into that port city,
Saint John's, to be exact.
Then came all the Liberty briefs
to encourage us on how to act.

We purchased souvenirs, saw sights,
and some had a buffet for lunch.
We quenched our thirst with

Tropical tea, "Tings," and a little rum punch.
And when it came time to bid farewell
to that tropical island fair,
we weighed anchor and manned the rail
as the ships whistle resounded through the air.

A brief stop in Puerto Rico
was made on the way back,
to pick up the ATG riders
and join us on our North-Northwest track.

SHREVEPORT passed the FEP
we can all gladly say,
with a sufficient list of discrepancies
incurred along the way.

More fun for the crew was planned
on our speedy homeward trek.
A Steel Beach Picnic took place
right there on the Flight Deck.

Of frowns and dejection
there was not a trace,
because the laughter escalated
with each pie in the face.

The Boxing Smoker
allowed shipmates to duke it out.
The best men were victorious,
surely, without a doubt.

And now our journey is ending
like the path of the evening sun,
to return us safely to port

and the greeting of our loved ones.
So bless us now, dear Lord,
until we set sail again.
Let all of Norfolk know
that SHREVPORT is pulling in!

Amen.

-14-

FLEET WEEK
Fun and favor in New York City

My first experience with Fleet Week was back in May of 1995, when I was still a Chaplain Candidate—still struggling with the dilemma of remaining as a local parish pastor or becoming an Active Duty Navy Chaplain.

I took a set of temporary duty orders to the Naval Amphibious Base in Little Creek, Virginia. Since it was only an hour drive from Richmond, I had planned to drive to the base and come home each evening. The first day, I checked in with the PHIBGRU2 chaplain to see where I would be assigned. He linked me up with a subordinate chaplain, who would serve as my mentor during the training. He proceeded to give me a tour of Little Creek as well as the Naval Station in Norfolk. While driving around the station, he received a call from the PHIBGRU2 chaplain. He paused, turned toward me, and asked, "Have you ever been to Fleet Week?"

"No, Sir. What is Fleet Week?" I asked.

He repeated my answer to the command chaplain. I became suspicious at this point and started to piece things together: *I had never been to Fleet Week. There are ships heading there. Would you like to go?*

"Ensign Brown," my mentor said as he paused the phone conversation. "There is a ship from our command leaving for Fleet Week today. You will be up there for about ten days. Do you want to go?"

It sounded exciting, almost too good to be true. Then I thought, *Hello! Your wife is expecting you to come home tonight.*

"Sir, how much time do I have to decide?"

"About five minutes. The ship leaves at noon and we need an answer ASAP!"

I was stressed! This was the first big impulsive decision in my marriage. I decided to go for it anyway.

"Yes, Sir. I will go."

"Good." He repeated my answer into the phone. He stayed on the line for another thirty seconds to receive further instructions. Once the call was over, he informed me of the game plan: Head back to the Bachelor Officer's Quarters at Little Creek, gather up my gear, come back to pier, and get on board the USS NASSAU (LHA-4) bound for New York City.

Everything happened so fast that I did not get a chance to call my wife and let her know about the change in plans. As I boarded the ship, I made an urgent request of my sponsor to call my wife at work, tell her that I was heading for New York, and I would call her in a couple of days when I got there. The ship left on time and by late afternoon I was 100 miles out to sea somewhere off the eastern shore of Virginia.

Two days later, the entire crew was manning the rails in the Parade of Ships up the Hudson River. Our ship sailed past the Verrazano Narrows Bridge and slowly approached the Battery in downtown Manhattan. I was at parade rest taking in the whole experience. It was then I knew:

God wanted to show me the world and he was going to do it through the Navy.

That message was so clear I felt that I was no longer a Parish Pastor. *This* was my new parish.

From that experience, I knew that the Red Carpet Treatment—compliments of the people of New York—was waiting for every Sailor arriving. Our Summer White uniforms were our passport to complimentary subway rides, meals, tickets to Broadway shows, and ballgames. There was no way anyone could come to Fleet Week and not have a good time.

Since I was familiar with the area and the event, I offered myself as an unofficial tour guide to the officers who wanted to find their way around the city.

18 May 2001
0908
From: RB@HOME
To: CHAPS@SHREVEPORT
Subject: Good morning

I know that you are about to get underway. Just wanted to send my love and 100 percent support! Please know that my prayers are with you as you head to New York City.

The five things that I am most thankful for are:
God being the center of my life and our family
A wonderful husband and son
Our extended family
The Prayer of Jabez
God, for the great things he has done

Please pray for us while you are away. Take care and I will talk to you soon.

Love,
RB

From: CHAPS@SHREVEPORT
To: RB@HOME
Re: Good Morning

Praise God for you, Honey! We are a blessed family. To know Christ and to be able to share and speak about our spiritual lives is a quality that many marriages do not have. Let's keep it going!

The Lord gave me the "five things" list during my devotions. It is a great way to pause and count our blessings. It is also a reliable pick-me-up no matter what kind of day you are having.

We are actually transiting past Lynnhaven and heading out to sea. I will stay in touch and let you know about the email hours.

Love,
Chaps

I was a bit melancholy on this departure. It seemed like we just got back a few days ago and now we were underway again. Even though we were heading to Fleet Week and bound to have a terrific time, my heart was at home.

2155
Pilot House
"Ready, Chaps?"
"Ready, Boats!"
"TATTOO, TATTOO! LIGHTS OUT IN FIVE MINUTES! STAND BY FOR THE EVENING PRAYER."

New Strength

They that wait upon the Lord shall renew their strength.
They shall mount up with wings as an eagle.
They shall run and not get weary; they shall walk and not faint.[3]

Gracious Lord, we find ourselves underway, once again, being called upon to give our best in support of mission readiness. Being at sea is the only way to test our mettle as sailors. It is the lone grinding stone that keeps both the edge and tip of the spear sharp. The logic behind this is understood; repetition in training reduces hazards of shipboard life and makes better sailors. Also, whether we say so or not, our collective endeavor is to be the best at what we do.

There is a strand of irony, though, interwoven throughout the fabric of our profession. While being at sea undoubtedly prompts the best from us as sailors, there is a challenge that beckons from the home front. Our loved ones, in their desire to be the best spouses, parents, family men and women possible, simultaneously task us to give liberally from the heart. Accomplishing this while at sea is not an easy feat. On top of this is another hurdle. How do we become the best we can be—treating others and ourselves with respect and dignity?

Lord, the answer and admission are plain. Whether spoken or unspoken, given freely or with reluctance, it requires a strength that we do not possess. For if we did it would always be a cinch to balance and satisfy both worlds.

Lord, we need your strength tonight to renew and refresh our spirits, to wash away any anxiety or fatigue. Give us the will to turn to you for a power that empowers us to do and be the best we can on whatever front we may find ourselves.

---

[3] Isaiah 40:31

They that wait upon the Lord shall renew their strength.
They shall mount up with wings as an eagle.
They shall run and not get weary; they shall walk and not faint.[4]

Amen.

19 May
0538
From: RB@HOME
To: CHAPS@SHREVEPORT
Subject: Thankful

This morning I heard "Jesus, You're the Center of My Joy" on the radio and I started reflecting on all that has happened during the past year. Even though it has been difficult, with God's help, we made it through. Although we still have trials known and unknown yet to face, God will continue to bring us through. Our joy rests in Jesus, not in the situation or circumstance, but in the assurance that He's always in the midst of the trials that we face.

I am thankful for:
Jesus who died on the cross to save me
Our son who got a good night's sleep
Waking up this morning to see another day
For our family
Victory in Jesus

Keep us lifted up in prayer. Have a blessed day!

Love,
RB

---

[4] Isaiah 40:31

0718
From: CHAPS@SHREVEPORT
To: RB@HOME
Re: Thankful

It sounds like that song was played just for you! I read Psalm 138 this morning and it proved to be a major blessing. It talked about all the things for which we should give thanks to the Lord.

The skies are "pea soup" out here! Visibility is less than one mile, which as far as navigation goes might as well be zero. We are proceeding slowly down to Morehead City with a stopover this afternoon at Onslow Bay.

I am thankful for:
The joy of knowing Jesus
Our family
A peaceful night without an AMCROSS message
More influence due to the Jabez Prayer
Serving the Lord with gladness

Please say a prayer for me. NSAC is this morning at 0830 and I want the Lord to have complete control.

Love,
Chaps

"MUSTER ALL NSAC PARTICIPANTS IN THE CHIEF'S MESS AT 0830"

The Low Visibility Detail was called due to the heavy fog we encountered. The Boatswain Mate-of-the-Watch was responsible for giving a blast of the ship's whistle every two minutes to warn other ships of our location until the fog cleared and the detail was secured. The fog never cleared.

1012
From: RB@HOME
To: CHAPS@SHREVEPORT
Re: Thankful

How was NSAC this morning? I sure hope it went well. Anyway, the Lord continues to bless. Continue to pray for us. I hope that the fog clears up. Talk to you soon.

RB

"LUNCH FOR THE CREW!"

1348

From: CHAPS@SHREVEPORT
To: RB@HOME
Re: Thankful

NSAC went very well! People are becoming familiar with it and supporting it ship-wide. The only guys who did not show up were those on the Low Visibility Detail. Some more good news about the program is the PHIBGRU2 chaplain wants to present it at the CNO's workshop on retention. Please continue to pray. It sounds like the program is getting some "Jabez" exposure.

RP1 Bates came back today and they are putting him right to work. He is just in time to help me with worship services.

The fog still hangs in the sky and probably will not lift very much today. It is the Lord's sign to us to slow down and do things right.

My prayers are always with you both. Talk to you later.

Chaps

From: RB@HOME
To: CHAPS@SHREVEPORT
Re: Thankful

I may head home this weekend and even go to DC with Mom and Dad. I am still thinking about that one, though. It would be a nice change of pace.

Until the next email, talk to you soon!
Love,
RB

"SWEEPERS, SWEEPERS, MAN YOUR BROOMS! GIVE THE SHIP A GOOD SWEEP-DOWN BOTH FORE AND AFT. SWEEP-DOWN ALL LADDERWELLS, LADDERBACKS, AND PASSAGEWAYS! HOLD ALL TRASH AND GARBAGE ON STATION."

2150

When I reached the Pilot House, the Boatswain Mate-of-the-Watch was positioned under the lever that sounded the ship's whistle. According to the guidelines, the whistle had to be sounded every two minutes during the Low Visibility Detail. He sounded it one last time before "Tattoo", which gave me exactly two minutes to pray.

The Fog of Life

Gracious Lord, the fog—which met us this morning, remained proximal at anchorage, and escorts us through the night—is just one of the many possible climate conditions with which seafarers must contend.

The haze—which restricts vision and visibility causing us to second-guess and double-check our heading, perpetually blowing the ship's whistle—has become an unexpected and perhaps uninvited guest on our transit.

But we have seen this before and we know how to navigate and negotiate this common barometric hurdle. Besides, we employ the spinning and spanning vigilance of RADAR, the pinpoint tracking of GPS, the fail-safe mathematics of Dead Reckoning, and our experience. Armed with these instruments, we bet the ship against any hazards hidden in a blanket of fog we cannot peer beyond with our naked eye.

Lord, in the same way, the "fog of life" occasionally descends upon us obscuring our view until all we behold is the haze of personal confusion, doubt, worry, and anxiety. Sometimes it makes little difference whether we wait it out or move in another direction; the fog does not lift at all.

However, you have not left us helpless. You have given us tools that will keep us proceeding through life:
Prayer, the communication link with heaven itself
Praise, the vocal offering that reciprocates with joy
Worship, the communal exaltation of your nature and presence

Armed with these instruments, we can bet our lives against any hazards hidden in a blanket of fog that we cannot peer beyond with the eyes of our faith.
Guide us, Gracious Lord, through the fog—be it natural or circumstantial— safely on course and within your care.

Amen.

20 May
1342
From: CHAPS@SHREVEPORT

To: RB@HOME
Subject: Moored at Morehead

We are moored at Morehead City! We arrived today about 1230 and will stay overnight loading equipment. The beaches are nice and the port is pretty clean. It looks like the downtown area is about one and one-half miles away and the crew is still waiting to see if the captain will allow Liberty this evening. If so, I will get to the closest phone and call you.

We had a good service aboard ship today. Fifteen sailors showed up. That is a pretty decent turnout, but the big thing is that people are becoming freer in the Spirit. They are starting to openly praise the Lord on their own. Before, it was as quiet as a mouse. Now, they enjoy singing the praise songs and you know that is right up my alley! God is moving and expanding His territory aboard ship.

5THINGS

I am thankful for Jesus and the presence of the Holy Spirit.
I am thankful for the way you persevere as a mom.
I am thankful for the strength of our marriage.
I am thankful for our son.
I am thankful for God's care, protection, and peace.
I will call you tonight as soon as I get off the ship. Try to get some rest.

Love,
Chaps

The captain granted Liberty later in the afternoon and directed "Beer on the Pier" for sailors who wanted to stay on the ship. Most of crew took advantage of Liberty, with the exception of those assisting with the on-load of Marines and their equipment. Deck Department and the Combat Cargo Officer are always tasked with something during these on-load evolutions.

About 1600

I thought about venturing out into Morehead City to search for dinner. From the ship I could see several seafood restaurants on the inlet side of the city. I had a dilemma: either have a good sit down meal in town or free burgers and barbeque on the ship. Tonight, "free" won. Still, I found a public phone at the end of the pier to call my wife. Then, I followed through with my intention to see the downtown area. By the time I returned to the ship, the Marines and their equipment were all embarked.

"THE UNDERWAY CHECK-OFF LIST IS POSTED ON THE QUARTERDECK."

21 May
0641
From: RB@HOME
To: CHAPS@SHREVEPORT

Re: Moored at Morehead

Good morning! Our son slept very well. He woke up just a couple of times. I am tired, but doing well.

5THINGS

New life through Jesus Christ
A good night's rest
The comfort that God provides when we go through trials
The love of family and friends
God being my refuge and strength

May God continue to provide his richest blessings upon our family and this household. Have a blessed day at sea!

Love,
RB

1414
From: CHAPS@SHREVEPORT
To: RB@HOME

Re: Moored at Morehead

We are getting ready to pull away from Morehead City. It was a good break to get away from the ship and onto dry land.

5THINGS

I am thankful for my salvation.
My family—all of them!
An evening off the ship
The power of the Prayer of Jabez
Talking to you on the phone

I will contact you sometime this afternoon. Give our son a hug and kiss for me. Have an abundantly blessed day!

Love,
Chaps

About 1500

Now that we were underway, we were making 20 knots for New York City. I made a request to the XO to do a 1MC announcement about the Community Relations projects lined up in New York. Once the XO gave the green light, I proceeded to design, print, and post the sign-up sheets on the starboard side AFT bulkhead on the Mess Deck. Shortly afterwards, I went back to the Pilot House to make the announcement:

"Onboard Shreveport, this is the chaplain. Let me have your attention for a moment. There will be several COMREL projects offered in New York City. There are sign-up sheets posted on the Mess Deck, starboard side AFT. If you sign up to participate, you will be expected to be present. That is all."

I made my way back down to the Mess Deck to see the response. It was quite good! Some were heading to the Youth Home, some to the hospital, and others to the Special Olympics.

About 2000
From: RB@HOME
To: CHAPS@SHREVEPORT
Subject: Some Sad News

I got a call from Mrs. Bolton in Memphis, Tennessee. Reverend Bolton's oldest son died. It was an accident. I believe they were loading tree logs onto one of those big trucks and one of the tree trunks fell off the truck and crushed him. He died instantly. Mrs. Bolton said that Reverend Bolton is doing as well as can be expected but was probably holding in his grief. I think he was with his son when it happened, which makes it even more difficult to bear. Please pray for his family and comfort for all. Mrs. Bolton said that the funeral would take place on Wednesday. Please continue to pray for us and say a special prayer for the Bolton Family.

Love,
RB

Reverend Bolton was the pastor of Noah Chapel AME Church in Millington, Tennessee, whom I met back in February 2000. I was on business for the Navy and my temporary duty extended over a weekend so I looked in the phone book to search for an AME church to attend. Noah Chapel was about six miles from the base.

The building itself was small, perhaps able to hold 100 people inside the sanctuary. I wore civilian clothes so that I could be anonymous. A few members greeted me as I entered the sanctuary and I took a seat in the back. The first thing I noticed was the hymnals directly in front of me were in poor shape. They were red and most likely out of print. The current AME hymnals were blue. To my surprise, they were not even AME hymnals. They were from the United Methodist Church, most likely donated. Just then, the Holy Spirit told me,

Purchase new hymnals for this church.

After service, I told Reverend Bolton what I planned to do. At first, he seemed grateful but a bit skeptical. He was quite surprised when about a month later UPS delivered several boxes to the door of the church filled with fifty brand new AME Church hymnals. I never mentioned this story to other pastors for the fear that they would invite me to their church so the Holy Spirit could "speak" to me there too.

Reverend Bolton was a sincere man and his wife was kind and hospitable. Losing a son is a difficult thing. I continued to pray for them with the other believers at the Daily Prayer Meeting.

Prepare

Gracious Lord, in the midst of transit to New York, all hands aboard SHREVEPORT—sailors and Marines—are making preparations to show ourselves and our ship to be at the pinnacle of presentation. While we continue to prepare for our arrival, help us to consider this:
Let us prepare to meet with you. Taking the time to sweep clean all the ladder backs, bulkheads, angle irons, and storage chambers of our hearts; our preparatory actions should remind us that meeting with you is a sacred, intimate event.

Let us prepare to hear you. There is no electronic assistance required, just a heart that is open, willing, silent, and still. That is the correct frequency needed to tune in to your voice.

Let us prepare to place our faith in you. Before the sandman brings sleep to our eyes or the Watchmen rise to their nocturnal post, we place our very lives and the care of our loved ones in your Omnipotent hands.

Let us prepare to serve you. With gladness, let our service to you reflect the gratitude for so many blessings in our lives and extend clearly, openly towards all of our shipmates.

Let us prepare a way that is pleasing to you. For "all our ways are in full view and you examine all our paths."[5] Help us to take an accurate account of our lives that is measured by your "yardstick" and not the shifting scales of our relative morality.

In all our diligent and detailed preparation let us never forget to place the same energy—or greater—into preparing to seek you.

Amen.

"TAPS, TAPS, LIGHTS OUT! ALL HANDS TURN TO YOUR BUNKS. MAINTAIN SILENCE ABOUT THE DECKS. TAPS!"

22 May
0622
From: RB@HOME
To: CHAPS@ SHREVEPORT
Subject: Good morning

Hey!

I hope the seas were calm for you. We had a really big storm hit us overnight that came out of nowhere. They are expecting more thunderstorms later today. Continue to pray for us and keep the Bolton family in your prayers too.

---

5 Proverbs 5:21

5THINGS

The fact that God is greater than any problem I face
Waking up with a sound mind, body, and spirit
A loving and caring husband and son
God's comfort in time of grief
God's love

Have a blessed day!
RB

0802
From: CHAPS@SHREVEPORT
To: RB@HOME
Re: Good Morning

Even though the news about Rev. Bolton's son has put a damper on my day,
I am still pressing forward. I guess the measure of our faith is how we react
to difficult circumstances. My prayers are with them and I will lift his entire
family up at today's prayer meeting.

5THINGS

I am thankful for being alive today.
I am thankful for Jesus carrying me when I am tired.
I am thankful for how He sustains you every day.
I am thankful for the ministry aboard this ship.
I am thankful for being one day closer to you.
It is time for another NSAC Class. I will write back later.

Chaps

1301
From: RB@HOME
To: CHAPS@SHREVEPORT
Re: Good Morning

Please let me know if you will need ATM money once you arrive. I will also wait for your call when you get into port.

Talk to you soon.
Luv,
RB

"SWEEPERS, SWEEPERS, MAN YOUR BROOMS! GIVE THE SHIP A GOOD SWEEPDOWN BOTH FORE AND AFT. SWEEPDOWN ALL LADDERWELLS, LADDERBACKS, AND PASSAGEWAYS; HOLD ALL TRASH AND GARBAGE ON STATION."

1503
From: CHAPS@SHREVEPORT
To: RB@HOME
Re: Good morning

The rest of the day was spent cleaning the ship. RP1 Bates and I have a little more to do in our spaces and then we will quit for the evening.

I am okay as far as money is concerned. If I do need to use the ATM, I will let you know and how much. There are a whole lot of things that are free for sailors in New York City. Reveille is super early tomorrow—0430—and we make our procession into New York Harbor around 0645. I will get the same guy who took my picture while we were coming back from Antigua to get some good shots on the way into port.

5THINGS

I am thankful for the joy of Jesus.
I am thankful for all the love and support you provide.
I am thankful for being able to call you soon.
I am thankful for twenty-four-hour email access.
I am thankful for the way God is growing your life.
Lord's blessings upon you both.

Love,
Chaps

"TATTOO, TATTOO! LIGHTS OUT IN FIVE MINUTES! STAND BY FOR THE EVENING PRAYER."

Fleet Week Arrival

Gracious Lord, we rejoice tonight on the brink of our arrival in New York City. We have worked so hard as a crew to get to this point and we are looking forward to what lies ahead. For now, done are the wet swabs, waxed floors, and scrubbed ladder backs. Buckets of "haze gray" paint have been applied. Uniforms—whites and "Charlies"—have been cleaned and pressed and are set for presentation. We are ready to enjoy Liberty in the international capital of the world.

They are ready for us too.

The red carpet treatment begins as each ship crosses under the Verrazano Narrows Bridge; Fort Hamilton will herald each vessel with a gun salute as it passes. Lord, Fleet Week offers us unlimited prospects for recreation and enjoyment.

*We are so blessed to belong to a nation that thinks so highly of us that it
throws such a celebration in our honor. It is a privilege that befits the greatest
Navy that ever sailed the seas. Lord, we praise you for this much needed break,
a Liberty breather that should allow us to unwind and recharge our batteries.
During the next seven days, let us take this opportunity to thank you for the
blessings we enjoy "gratis" due to our citizenship and in a much bigger way,
to your grace and mercy so abundantly shed upon our lives.*

Amen.

23 May
Sometime after Breakfast

I looked outside the ship and the same fog that greeted us at the mouth
of the Chesapeake Bay was here in New York Harbor. The fog was so thick it
canceled the Parade of Ships. I was disappointed because the parade was the
highlight of the Fleet Week celebration. I remember how much I enjoyed
the parade when I experienced it for the first time back in 1995 aboard the
USS NASSAU (LHA-4). The entire crew manned the rails of the ship as it
sailed past the Battery, the Trade Towers, all the way up to the cruise ship
terminals in midtown Manhattan. We moored right next to the Intrepid
Sea, Air, and Space Museum—but not this time, not this year.

From: CHAPS@SHREVEPORT
To: RB@HOME
Subject: Good morning from New York!

Hi Honey!

We are pulling into New York City but we cannot see a thing due to heavy
fog, which has visibility down to one-half of a mile. The parade of ships up
the Hudson River has been cancelled so that means we will be coming into
port three hours early. I will give you a call as soon as I can get off the ship.
I am continuing to pray for your strength.

Love,
Chaps

0640
From: RB@HOME
To: CHAPS@SHREVEPORT
Re: Good morning from New York

Welcome to the Big Apple! I am glad you arrived safely. We are doing fine. I think that I may go home to see my folks this weekend to break up the routine. I will probably leave on Friday and return on Tuesday to avoid traffic.

5THINGS

The unconditional love of God
The undying love of God
The presence of the Holy Spirit
The abilities with which God has blessed me
God placing you and our son in my life
Have fun in New York City. Hope to talk to you soon.

Love,
RB

1020
From: CHAPS@SHREVEPORT
To: RB@HOME
Re: Good morning from New York

We are docked in Staten Island at Sullivan's Pier! I will be getting off the ship for lunch and heading to the chaplain's reception at the Seaman's Church Institute around 3:00 p.m. Look for a call mid-afternoon.

Love,
Chaps

Our mooring position at the pier placed us beside the USS BARRY (DDG-58). There were several other ships that I did not recognize by name. I was envious of all the "lucky dogs", whom got to moor in mid-town Manhattan like the USS JOHN F. KENNEDY (CV-67). Still, we received a very warm welcome from the people of Staten Island. They set up tents with refreshments such as coffee, danish, doughnuts, etc. There were brochures, maps, and discounted tickets—everything from baseball games to Broadway shows. I even spotted some veterans from the local VFW (Veterans of Foreign Wars) wearing their command post garrison covers. They too greeted the sailors as they came ashore.

The Seaman's Church Institute was hosting a reception for all the chaplains participating in Fleet Week. Chaplain Gregg Todd, the Command Chaplain from the US Coast Guard Station in Staten Island, emailed me an invitation during our transit to New York. He picked me up at the pier along with Chaplain Scott Morton from the BARRY. He provided us with a quick tour of the Father Cappadano Memorial Chapel and then we headed for the reception.

When we arrived, there were four or five other Navy chaplains and a host of civilian clergy present, most of whom were associated with the institute. Everyone was extremely cordial towards us and appreciative of our presence. A few queried us; quite fascinated by the stories we shared about ministry-at-sea and shipboard life.

There were numerous trays of heavy hors-d'oeuvres and plenty of bottles of alcohol. I do not drink but there were many ministers who had a glass of wine and other mixed drinks to accompany their meal. Nothing was done in excess, though. In my denomination, ministers who drank socially were sometimes referred to as "sipping saints." We finally met the director of the institute, who greeted us, shared the history and purpose of the institute, and provided a "nickel" tour of building. Chaplain Todd drove us back to the ship at the conclusion of the evening.

Over the next few days, the fog gave way to copious rain showers that cancelled many of the scheduled events. Still, we were able to send a contingent of sailors to the COMREL project at the youth home in Brooklyn. The sailors had a great time and the young people were so impressed with them that they wanted the sailors to stay longer so they could learn more about the Navy.

With no further duties aboard ship, I decided to put in Leave and head home for a few days to visit my family. I called my brother, who was able to pick me up at the Cranford Rail Station. I returned on Saturday evening in order to prepare for Sunday services. It was agreed that worship services would be held at the chapel adjacent to the pier rather than conduct individual services aboard each ship. When Sunday morning came, I was not expecting a large crowd. We were on Liberty in New York City and for most sailors and Marines today was not a day of worship. It was just the morning after Saturday night out on the town.

I met Chaplain Morton outside of the chapel at 1045 and offered to serve as his assistant worship leader. He brought along a Lay Leader from the BARRY to assist as well. There were a total of four sailors in attendance, including myself, at the service.

I came back to the pier later in the day to attend the Sunset Parade. The US Marine Corps Drum and Bugle Corps performed for the crowd gathered followed by a performance by the US Marine Silent Drill Platoon. They were outstanding—"razor blade" sharp and "baby-bottom" smooth! Watching all their flawlessly synchronized marching and movements made me proud to be an American.

27 May
Memorial Day
1200

At noon on the pier in front of SHREVEPORT and BARRY, the Memorial Day Service of Remembrance was scheduled. On the stage was the Commanding Officer from the BARRY, who was invited to offer brief remarks, and a congressman from Staten Island, who brought his elementary-aged son with him. The congressman was born and raised on Staten Island and seemed to be a "favorite son" for his district.

The audience was a good mix of civilian and military. I was invited to offer the Invocation and a local Catholic priest did the Benediction.

Let us pray.

Sovereign God, we thank you for this opportunity to pause, reflect, and honor the men and women who willingly gave their lives in service to their country. Though the innumerable monuments and cemeteries mark their sacrifice across the world, we who are gathered at this specific place and time, desire to be reminded of the precious price they paid on our behalf. We also realize that freedom understands one price: the shedding of blood. And it seems that in today's hostile world there is a running tab with an increasing demand for more.

We owe so much to our fallen brothers and sisters; it is a debt we can never repay. The best currency we can dispense is to never forget them: to tell this generation, the next, and even those unborn that America honors its dead, taken in the heat and horror of battle. We as a people, shall always find the will to remember no matter how difficult those memories may be. Let it be forever understood that we love those who have left this world so that those who remain can carry the banner of freedom for another day. Grant us, Lord, the courage to hold it high and proud.

Amen.

28 May
Out to Dinner

Doc and Dental Doc were not my usual Liberty buddies but I had bragged to them that I knew where to get the best burger in the city.

"It is called the Silver Spur," I told them. "Located on 8th Avenue and Broadway."

They were interested in trying it so we took the Staten Island Ferry to Lower Manhattan, located the subway, hopped the "A" train, and headed uptown.

The train was a bit crowded and seats were few so I decided to stand and allow my colleagues to sit. There was a woman who noticed us in uniform and struck up a conversation.

"We are here for Fleet Week, Ma'am," we answered.

"Oh! Well, where are you guys stationed?"

"Norfolk, Virginia," I replied for the group.

"How do you like the city?" she asked.

I let Doc and Dental Doc respond first since the city was so familiar to me.

When we mentioned that we were going out to get some dinner, she seemed very interested in where we were heading.

"We are going to a restaurant called the Silver Spur. It is on 8th and Broadway," I said.

"The Silver Spur, what kind of food do they serve there?"

"Well, we are going for the burgers. They have some of the best in the city."

"Burgers?" she inquired with a twinge of disdain. "Wouldn't you rather have something else? I know this great restaurant in Soho..."

She proceeded to tell us of some place that sounded very "healthy". As she began to mention another place, I perceived that she was a Vegan so our "burger" response must have made her think that we did not know what we were doing. She probably could not fathom coming all the way into the city just to pick up a burger.

"Yes!" she concluded with confidence. "You guys ought to give those places a try."

"Wow! Gee, thanks Ma'am," we responded but our hearts and body language subtly said something different. Besides, I already made up my mind where I was going to eat tonight and it was not at some trendy Vegan place in Soho. Doc was a "carnivore" too, even a skilled deer hunter from Pennsylvania so I know what he wanted for dinner. As for Dental Doc, well, he was from Tennessee.

We departed the train at our stop and headed topside for the streets. It was a short walk over to the restaurant form there. The first thing I noticed was that they remolded the whole place since I last ate there in the late

1980's. It now had a retro-Streamliner look with stainless steel chairs, table leg fittings, and checkerboard vinyl flooring.

My favorite burger, known as the Ten Gallon Hat, had changed names but was still the same delicious big-beef burger that it was years ago—smothered with Jack Cheese, bacon, mushrooms, lettuce, tomatoes, and barbeque sauce with large dill pickle spears and steak fries on the side. The two docs ordered something different but both were very impressed with the size and satisfied with the taste of their choices.

"This is pretty good, Chaps," said Doc.

"Yeah, what a burger!" exclaimed Dental Doc.

Our waitress came over and asked, "Desert?"

"No thanks. We are stuffed!"

Doc took a moment to look over the menu to find the alcoholic beverage offerings.

"What kind of wine do you have?" he asked.

Wine, Doc? I thought, *At a burger joint?*

But that was Doc. In spite of our mundane setting and the meal of which we partook, he asked to see the wine list. To his credit, though, Doc was bit of a wine connoisseur. Back home in Pennsylvania, he grew up with a wine cellar stacked with various vintages. He could easily discern a good glass from a poor one. He ended up choosing one that cost five dollars, which he said tasted "about five bucks."

Once we finished our meal, we walked for a bit and then caught the train and ferry back to the ship.

29 May
Day Trip: World Trade Center

Both Dental Doc and Lieutenant Dull wanted to see the World Trade Center but did not know how to get there. They were specifically interested in going to the Observation Deck. I was a bit skeptical because the weather was so overcast this morning. Visibility would be next to impossible. However, they seemed persistent about their desire to try. We left the ship later that morning with the hope that the extra time would allow the weather to clear. It did, but slowly.

It was about lunchtime so we decided to grab a bite on the streets. My preference was to have "eating plans" before I left in a group because it is hard to come to a consensus once we are on the streets. Somehow, we ended up in Chinatown and from there it was "take your pick." Every block had four to five restaurants and the menus started to all look the same. We finally came to a decision and ate.

Lunch allowed enough time for the skies to clear. A brilliant dome of sunshine began to prevail, which made it a sure bet for good viewing at the Observation Deck. Someone mentioned that they wanted to try to get some good deals on tickets that the USO (United Service Organization) was offering to sailors. That meant another subway trip uptown to the Penn Station Bus Terminal.

When we arrived, they offered us free refreshments, souvenirs, and discounted tickets. However, the sailors from the KENNEDY snatched all the best deals. That was the advantage to being moored in Manhattan: first dibs on *all* the great deals.

When we got back on the subway, I made sure we got off at a station a few blocks from the towers. When we emerged, both Dental Doc and Lieutenant Dull stared straight up, amazed at the sight.

"Wow, Chaps! Wow!" exclaimed Lieutenant Dull.

"Awesome sight, Man!" said Dental Doc.

I let them stand and stare so they could soak up the moment.

"Yep, that's it. And we are going to the top," I said.

We began to walk over to the plaza between the towers when I saw the sculpture "The Sphere," by Fritz Koenig. I did a research paper on it in my Contemporary Art class back in college. We walked inside the South Tower and found the elevators that would take us 110 stories straight up to the Observation Deck. The elevator whizzed us upward so fast that it gave the sensation of being slightly weightless.

The view from the Observation Deck was spectacular! Tens-of-miles of unrestricted visibility: to the south, the Battery, Governor's Island, Statue of Liberty, Verazzano Narrows Bridge, Bayonne, Staten Island and beyond. To the east we could see all of Brooklyn, Queens, and the rest of Long Island. Looking north, all of Manhattan was clear past the Empire State Building and George Washington Bridge. To the west, we saw Jersey City, Newark Airport, and northern New Jersey out to the mountains at the western part of the state.

Many of the people on the observation deck were tourists, perhaps from France and Germany with others of Asian descent. Cameras and poses were plentiful. For Dental Doc, it was his first time at the top and it did not disappoint.

Once back inside, Dental Doc mentioned that he heard Nathan's hot dogs were really good so he wanted to try this "New York" dog. I pointed him to the concession stand located in the lobby but privately thought, *if he really wanted the authentic experience, he needed to go out to "The Source" on Coney Island.*

We made it back down to the bottom floor when Lieutenant Dull and Dental Doc told me they wanted to head back to the ship. However, it was early in the evening and I wanted to head to Shea Stadium to see a Mets baseball game. I knew that I would be breaking the Liberty buddy rule but I reasoned that I knew the city well enough. I felt comfortable venturing on my own.

I searched for a bite to eat, passing by the escalators leading to the Path Trains. I reminisced about how often I had taken that trip home to New Jersey. It was crowded, about rush hour, and most of the places were packed. I decided to go to Sbarro's and get a slice of pizza. This was a brave proposition considering the red pizza sauce could make a very conspicuous stain on my Summer White uniform. The slice was as delicious as I was careful.

Before I got on the subway I decided to call my wife and give her an update on the day. Right in the middle of our conversation, a man stopped behind me and said, "Chaplain Brown?"

I turned and could not believe whom I saw: a former Marine Officer with whom I served in Twentynine Palms, California, Captain Mike Caunedo. We were good neighbors in base housing and fellow "Jerseyans".

I told my wife who just walked up and she agreed to cut our conversation short. Seeing him brought back many memories: days out in the field, forced marches with his Marines in the desert, and his white pit bull "Tyson". He was as surprised to see me, as I was to see him.

"Where did you go after Twentynine?" I asked.

"I did a few years at Camp Pendleton and got out. How about you?"

"Naval Training Center in Great Lakes and now I have done eight months aboard the USS SHREVEPORT."

"How is your wife doing?" I asked.

"She is great. In fact, we are expecting our first child."

"That is great!" I exclaimed.

"How about you?"

"Yes, a son who is a little over a year old. What do you do now?"

"I work here at the Trade Center for Goldman Sachs," he said.

"Man, I can't get over this. I am so glad you stopped and talked."

He and I exchanged numbers and emails and talked about getting together for lunch. Then we departed, he for the Path Train, and I for the subway.

From there, I was solo on the subway heading to the Mets game. Most people from out-of-town would not venture alone on the subway in New York City at night. However, I felt very safe in my uniform, during Fleet Week in New York City.

Shea Stadium

It was not hard to locate the sailors at the game for two reasons: first, all of our complimentary tickets were in the same section, second, find the "beer man" and there will be sailors nearby. Sure enough, there they were. Only in this instance, the "beer man" was not actually an employee of the stadium. He was some guy having a raucous good time with the sailors. At the very least, he had a beer buzz. From what I could tell his name was Pete. The sailors were laughing and joking along with him, which I thought was strange. *Why so chummy with a guy they just met?* Upon further observation, this man was treating each Sailor that showed up in our section to a beer just by shouting "P-e-e-e-t!" It seemed like he was trying to show his appreciation for sailors but it was obvious that they were taking advantage of his hospitality and lack of sobriety.

"You guys should not be doing this," I said raising my voice over the crowd.

"Come on, Sir. We are just having a good time. Besides, he offered."

"He is drunk! Can't you guys see that?" I pointed out.

Just then Pete called out to me, "Hey! Hey you, Sailor! You wanna beer?"

"Uh, no thanks," I said feeling slightly sorry for the guy.

The Mets were losing and it was getting late so I decided to head back to the ship.

"Hey, don't worry, Sir. We will take care of him," said one Sailor.

"Yeah, I bet you guys will. See you back at the ship."

As I left that row of seats and headed up the concrete steps, a few more sailors passed me headed down to our section. When I reached the top of the stairs, I heard faint shouts in the background, "P-e-e-e-t!"

"Sailors," I said under my breath, shaking my head.

30 May

Every uniformed Sailor that participated in Fleet Week had been offered a free viewing of the new movie, *Pearl Harbor*. It was being shown at a theater in midtown Manhattan. My Liberty buddies today would be Ensign (ENS) Luckie and First Lieutenant (1st LT) Adams. I heard the movie was about three hours long and I hoped that it would keep my interest. I knew that the subject matter would, but it also would depend on how the movie was portrayed. We arrived at the theater to a sea of white uniforms. Obviously, everyone got the word about the "price of admission."

Three Hours Later

The producers did a great job, especially with the special effects and flight scenes. The lingering thought afterwards was about the many people who lost their lives that day. I am glad that they included the story of Dory Miller, a Navy cook who was credited with shooting down several Japanese planes on that day. After the film, we headed back to the ship to take a break before heading out to dinner on our last night on the town.

About 1900

First Lieutenant Adams, Ensign Luckie, and I decided to go back into Manhattan to visit Times Square and look for dinner. The 1stLT had a tip on a good soul food restaurant called, The Shark Bar, supposedly located on 76th and Amsterdam Ave. That meant another trip on the "A" Train, heading uptown.

When we arrived at the location, the restaurant was nowhere in sight.

"1st, are you sure you have the right address?" asked Ensign Luckie.

"Yeah. It is the one they gave me on the ship," he said. "Maybe we could walk around the next couple of blocks and find it."

"Negative, 1st," I said. "If we try to 'just find' something in the city then we will just get further lost. Let's ask someone who looks local."

"Hey! Let's ask her," said ENS Luckie. He picked out a senior citizen taking her poodle for a walk.

"Yeah, she looks local," I said.

We approached her together but 1st LT spoke up for us.

"Excuse us, Ma'am, we are looking for a place called The Shark Bar. Do you happen to know where it is?"

"Well, let me see. The Shark Bar, you said, right?"

"Yes, Ma'am," answered 1st.

"Well, what address do you have for it?"

"Yes, Ma'am, we have 76th Street and Amsterdam Avenue," said 1st.

"And it is not there?" she asked.

"No, Ma'am. It is not."

"Okay. You said Amsterdam Avenue, right?"

"Yes, Ma'am, that is correct."

"Well, you know you are on Amsterdam Avenue right now."

"Uh, yes Ma'am, we do."

"Well, if I were you, I would head back down Amsterdam because I do not think that restaurant is this far north," she said.

It was no trouble to be patient with her. She was being very sweet to stop and try to help us out.

"Are you gentlemen in the Navy?" she asked.

"Yes, Ma'am, we are," we all answered.

"You must be here for Fleet Week, right?"

"Yes, Ma'am."

"Well, you look really sharp. Where are you from?" she asked.

One-by-one, we began to introduce ourselves. Ensign Luckie began and when he was done, 1st LT started. As I listened to him speak, I stepped out of the moment and began to feel really special.

There we stood: three clear-minded, Christian, African-American men, and naval officers in their crisp Summer White uniforms. It was a beautiful thing.

"Well, I want you all to know how proud I am that you are serving our country. It was a real privilege to meet you this evening."

"Thank you, Ma'am. We really appreciate your help," we told her.

"You are welcome. Just keep walking down Amsterdam. I am sure you will find it," she said.

We thanked her again, wished her "Good evening," and headed down the street. We crossed 75th Street and there it was to our left—The Shark Bar.

"Well, what do you know?" said 1st LT.

"Hey, Man. Whatever works," said ENS Luckie.

"I do not know about you guys but I am ready to eat," I said.

"Same here, Chaps" said 1st LT.

"Yeah, let's do this," said ENS Luckie.

We had a great meal and a great time. It took an hour-and-a-half to get back to the ship but it was definitely worth it.

"THE UNDERWAY CHECK-OFF LIST IS POSTED ON THE QUARTERDECK."

31 May
0543
From: RB@HOME

To: CHAPS@SHREVEPORT
Subject: Good morning

I guess by now you are gearing up to head home. I hope Fleet Week was a good break for you and the crew. It sounds like you had a great time.

5THINGS

Jesus intercedes for me.
God is always with me.
Our son
A good wake-up
Only two days left
Thanks again for your phone calls. They really help.

Love,
RB

From: CHAPS@SHREVEPORT
To: RB@HOME
Re: Good morning

Honey,

It was good to speak to you yesterday.

After we left the ferry station, we headed north for Times Square to do some souvenir shopping. Times Square is so lit up at night that it reminds me of the Las Vegas Strip, especially the Freemont Street Experience. Anyway, tourists from England, Japan, and India wanted to take pictures with us three. It is funny, even though there were a lot of sailors around it seemed like we were the most photogenic. Go figure?

We went further uptown and had dinner at a place called The Shark Bar. It is an African-American establishment on Amsterdam Avenue. The atmosphere was classy but not too formal and the food was absolutely out of this world! I asked our waitress how the restaurant got its name. It seems that during Prohibition, New York had small, illegal clubs called speakeasies, where you could relax after work and have drinks with your friends. The people who hung out at these establishments were called sharks, due to the daring act of drinking in the first place and then having to move in and out of these kinds of places. It was so refreshing to see "us" owning and operating something of this quality. Everyone was relaxed and congenial but attentive. Our waitress was a graduate of the Culinary Institute of America and was very bright and articulate. She seemed very ambitious and wants to open several restaurants all at the same time. 'Talk about a type A personality!

5THINGS

A great time in New York
Being able to visit with my family in New Jersey
The strength God continues to provide
Our family
Heading home

Love,
Chaps

P.S. – They just passed this morning that our arrival will be delayed by half a day. I know that does not sound great. The reason seems to be that there is a ship in Morehead City that will not be finished with their off-loading of material on Thursday when we get down there. This will force us to anchor off the coast until Friday morning. Then we can "dump and run" back up the coast for home. We should be back by mid-afternoon on Saturday.

Continue to pray because the news of the extra half day is not sitting well with the crew.

1116
From: RB@HOME
To: CHAPS@SHREVEPORT
Re: Good morning

It sounds like you had a really good time, especially on your last night in the Big Apple. Well, I guess we have to postpone the homecoming countdown by a half day. The main thing is that you are on your way.

Talk to you soon.

Love,
RB

1611
From: CHAPS@SHREVEPORT
To: RB@HOME

Hey!

Thanks for being so understanding about this weekend. You are right; the main thing is the safe return. I will give you more details as they develop.

I think we are somewhere off the coast of New Jersey, heading south at top speed. Our ship's store is having a big sale tonight on electronics. They have advertised "great prices" on cameras, DVDs, cassette players, etc. I will stop by to see how good the deals really are.

Have a great evening!
Chaps

2155

"TATTOO, TATTOO! LIGHTS OUT IN FIVE MINUTES! STAND BY FOR THE EVENING PRAYER."

Recuperation from Fleet Week

Gracious Lord, we thank you for all the great experiences and memories that were Fleet Week in New York City. We had such a great time that we are just a bit worn down from all the festivities. We have discovered, in New York there are more things to do than time in which to do them. What a privilege it was to experience first-hand the full hospitality of our hosts, the people of New York, who opened their hearts to us in so many different ways.

But now our attention has turned south to complete this mission. Lord, we are content; yet, there is a simmering anxiety to get home. Settle our hearts, focus our attention on our work, and keep us always trusting in you. In your Holy Name, we pray.

Amen.

01 June

"REVEILLE, REVEILLE! ALL HANDS HEAVE OUT! BREAKFAST FOR THE CREW!"

0610

From: RB@HOME

To: CHAPS@SHREVEPORT

Good morning, Chaps! How are you doing? We are getting ready to go out and run a few errands today.

5THINGS

God answers prayer.

God is faithful.

A good night's sleep

God's strength, which carries me through the day

The presence of God in our family

May you have a blessed day! Hope to hear from you soon.

Love,

RB

From: CHAPS@SHREVEPORT

To: RB@HOME

Re: Good morning!

I am glad you had a good night's rest. God does truly answer prayer. I am continuing to lift you up in prayer and, specifically, the Jabez prayer over your lives.

5THINGS

The presence and power of the Holy Spirit

Our wonderful family

The new horizons God continually places in our lives

One day closer to you

Just to be alive to serve the Lord another day

Please pray for my Aunt. Mom mentioned that she is undergoing medical treatments. Also, pray for a new class of NSAC sailors.

Love,

Chaps

Later in the day, the captain called for a special dinner meal in the Wardroom to honor the Marines. It was their last night on ship and he wanted to provide them with an appropriate send off. The Supply Officer brought out the white tablecloths and the good china and silverware. Steak and lobster were on the menu with pie a la mode for dessert. The captain gave the first remarks and made a special presentation to the commander of the Marines. The commander returned the gesture by offering the captain a gift as well.

Morehead City

It is a strange thing; the crew had a way of off-loading material and equipment at Morehead City a bit quicker than they do for an on-load. This was due to the fact that they knew the only thing standing between them and heading home—today—was getting the Marines and their gear off the ship. They did so safely and efficiently and by late afternoon we proceeded out of the Bogue Sound and into open waters heading for home.

The Last Leg of the Journey

Gracious Lord,
Until our reunion has begun,
we cannot rest our hands 'til the work is done.
Keep us vigilant this night through the rising the sun,
on the last leg of the journey.

Before our plans for the weekend come to fruition
or the ship rests at its mooring position,
give us the resolve to complete this mission
on the last leg of the journey.

Twelve hours ahead of us Pier 22 awaits,
but there is a Navigation Plan we must negotiate.
Keep the Watch alert and ready to concentrate,

on the last leg of the journey.

Our loved ones back home have been patient beyond measure.
Their care for us while at sea has been our own private treasure.
Let us meet again for that extended moment of leisure,
on the last leg of the journey.

Lord, we are so thankful you have kept us safe these past fourteen days,
from Morehead City's tranquility to New York Harbor's haze.
Your tender loving care for us will never cease to amaze,
even on the last leg of the journey.

Amen.

"TAPS, TAPS, LIGHTS OUT! ALL HANDS TURN TO YOUR BUNKS. MAINTAIN SILENCE ABOUT THE DECKS. TAPS!"

02 June
0620
From: CHAPS@SHREVEPORT
To: RB@HOME
Subject: Coming in a bit early

Hey!

We are coming in a bit earlier than originally planned. Instead of arriving at noon we will be pier side at 1045. This will put me home around 1230-1300. Praise the Lord for the change to the schedule!

5THINGS

God's sustaining grace
The Prayer of Jabez

The tremendous job you have done at home
Just thirteen hours left on this trip
Our family
Talk to you soon (face to face)
Chaps

From: RB@HOME
To: CHAPS@SHREVEPORT
Re: Coming in a bit early

I praise God that He is bringing you home early! Cannot wait to see you.

5THINGS

God hears and answers the prayers of his people.
God continues to sustain me and give me strength when you are not here.
That you had a wonderful time in NYC
A safe journey home
You will be home in a little while.

Love ya and see you soon
RB

"SET CONDITION 1-ALPHA FOR WELL DECK OPERATIONS! SET CONDITION 1-ALPHA FOR WELL DECK OPERATIONS!"

0739
From: CHAPS@SHREVEPORT
To: RB@HOME
Re: Coming in a bit early

Hi Honey!

We are coming up on our turn at Cape Henry Lighthouse in Virginia Beach. As soon as we drop off the LCU at Little Creek, we are headed into port. We will be at Pier 22 instead of Pier 3. They are providing shuttle service for us so we can get back to our cars.

5MORE THINGS

Jesus
Coming home early
Coming home to a wonderful family
Coming home to a wonderful home
Coming home

See you in five hours!

Chaps

FIREMAN WHITE
Losing our best and brightest

08 July 2001

I just completed a Sunday morning worship service aboard ship when a Sailor stopped me in the passageway to tell me that First Lieutenant Adams was looking for me. He was the Command Duty Officer for the day, which probably meant there was a request for counseling or something that required my attention. I went out to the Quarterdeck to meet him but he was not there. The Petty Officer of the Watch said the he was out on the Flight Deck making a phone call.

He was still on the phone as I approached him. He finished the call and broke the news. "Hey, Chaps. One of our sailors was shot and killed last night while he was on Leave. It was Machinist Mate Fireman Patrick White. Do you know who he was?" asked 1ˢᵗ LT.

"No, I can't think of him right now." I responded. I was shocked at the news but for the life of me I could not picture this Sailor.

"He was that new Sailor—African-American—who worked in the Wardroom as a Food Service Assistant. You know, the quiet kid with good manners," said 1ˢᵗ.

"Yes. Yes! I know him. Oh my Gosh! How did it happen?"

"We do not know all the details yet but it happened in his hometown in South Carolina," he said.

"Have the CO and XO been notified?"

"Yes, I called them." 1st stopped abruptly because he was getting another call on the cell.

"Chaps, let me take this call. It is Fireman White's sister. She is stationed over at Little Creek."

"Sure 1st. Do what you need to do," I said.

My shock began to mix with anger. *Another one of our young lives snuffed out—for what?* Even though I did not know all the circumstances behind the shooting, I had this gnawing feeling that it was over something foolish.

An administrative process took place upon the death of a service member: assignment of a Casualty Assistance Call Officer (CACO), collection of the service member's personal effects from the ship, a memorial service for the crew to honor his life, a Letter of Condolence from the CO to the primary next of kin. The problem was that all this had to be accomplished very quickly because the ship was scheduled to get underway in less than 48 hours.

09 July

The captain decided to hold the memorial service this morning about an hour after Quarters. He announced the news to the crew, who by now, had already heard about Fireman White's death through word-of-mouth. RP1 Bates and I had to scramble a bit to get things together—he for the logistical setup, the program, and bulletin and I for the memorial reflection. The captain also decided to send me down to South Carolina rather than an officer or chief from Fireman White's division. I suspect through me he wanted a "two-for-one"—command representation and pastoral care for the family.

I departed about midday heading south on Interstate 95. Fireman White was from a small town near Santee, South Carolina, which was about a six hour drive from Norfolk. All the way down my thoughts were for the grieving family.

It would have been one thing if he was killed in the line of duty
but in his hometown on Leave?
Why?

He had only been in the Navy for five months and SHREVEPORT was his very first assignment. It was more than tragic. It seemed stupid and senseless. However, I did not have all the facts yet so it was impossible to make a clear judgment about the situation.

When I arrived at the hotel in Santee, I checked in at the front desk, went back to my car to grab my bags, and then headed for my room. I established contact with the CACO from the Naval Weapons Station in Charleston, Chief Master-At-Arms (MAC) Mullen. He had been assigned to provide casualty assistance support to the family of Fireman White. He told me that he already paid a visit to the family and I told him that I was planning to do the same in the morning.

11 July
Mid-Morning

Yesterday's visit went as well as could be expected. Before I headed back to the family's house today, I wanted to provide the captain with an update while the ship was underway.

From: CHAPS@SC
To: CO@SHREVEPORT
Subject: Update from South Carolina

Sir,

I wanted to give you a preliminary update on the events concerning Fireman White's family and funeral arrangements:

- I made the first visit to their house yesterday morning at 1000 and met the parents and siblings of Fireman White, who were understandably distraught.

- I sat down privately with his mother and stepfather and presented them a copy of your Letter of Condolence, a copy of the memorial service bulletin, photos of the memorial service, and provided an explanation of the service—length, number of attendees, and comments made by you and others.
- Mrs. Clark, Fireman White's mother, thanked me for the explanation and expressed her appreciation for the service. Then I presented the ship's flag to the parents. The presentation of the flag stirred up their emotions but they still appreciated that we went to such lengths for their son.
- The Naval Weapons Station in Charleston dispatched MAC Darren Mullen as the CACO. He paid a visit to the family on Monday morning, however, a chaplain did not assist him. I tried to make contact with MAC Mullen yesterday but was unsuccessful. He is supposed to return to the family's home today and I will speak to him about further funeral arrangements.
- In the absence of a chaplain from Charleston, the family has requested that I participate in the wake on Friday evening at 1900 and the funeral on Saturday at 1400. Of course, I obliged and offered any further assistance.

I pray all is well with SHREVEPORT. I will continue to minister and meet the needs of Fireman White's family here in South Carolina.

Very respectfully,
Chaplain Brown

Late Afternoon

The Naval Weapons Station in Charleston got it right. MAC Mullen was a perfect choice to send as CACO to this family! I watched him patiently explain to Fireman White's parents all the survivor benefits associated with a service member's death. He also had great people skills, which made it easy to establish a rapport with Fireman White's family members and neighbors.

He definitely paved the way for me to attend to any deeper pastoral care needs, making my job a lot easier.

I returned to the hotel anxiously wanting to change out of my uniform because it only compounded the perspiring effect of Carolina's summer heat and humidity. Besides, I brought just two sets of uniforms—Summer and Service Dress Whites—and I wanted to keep them as tidy as possible. Sailors understand that these uniforms, though stunningly "Navy," are dust and smudge magnets requiring constant laundering maintenance.

15 July
Naval Amphibious Base in Little Creek, Virginia
From: CHAPS@NABLC
To: CO@SHREVEPORT
Subject: Mission accomplished!

Sir,

I returned this morning at 0100 from South Carolina safe and sound. Here is my final update:

- I spent the rest of the week visiting the family of Fireman White and assisting them in funeral arrangements, preps, and ministry of presence.
- It seems that MAC Mullen could not provide an explanation other than "I was the only CACO sent," as to the absence of a chaplain from the Naval Weapons Station in Charleston. My being there was providential in more ways than one.
- The wake, which was scheduled for 1900 on Friday, actually started early about 1830. Fireman White is from a small, rural, close-knit community in South Carolina where everyone is either related or knows each other very well. People, young and old, kept filing through the doors for the two hours paying their respects to the family and catching one last look at "Pat-Pat." Also, I presided over

the closing of the wake per the family's request. The service was concluded with scripture, prayer, and talking with remaining guests.

- The family was under a lot of stress by the time of the funeral on Saturday, which was understandable. By 1330, MAC Mullen had the honor guard in place at the cemetery. The service began on time and was well attended—about 400 people in a standing-room only sanctuary. Suffice to say, the overall mood was hard and sad. Most were at a loss to connect this good kid with such a wicked, senseless act. My remarks were made on your behalf and that of SHREVEPORT. I told them about the memorial service last Monday followed by some pastoral and personal comments to the family. The service ended with a final viewing of Fireman White and an eighty-car procession to the cemetery.

- During the committal, Fireman White received the customary Twenty-one Gun Salute and flag presentation. Afterwards, I met the family members and guests at a reception held at the house. MAC Mullen, who did an excellent job taking care of all CACO concerns, was there too. I said farewell and left my address and phone number. I reassured them, if there was anything we could do in the future to call us immediately.

- Justice update: The county sheriff has apprehended three of the four alleged suspects—one being the "trigger man"—involved in the shooting. It seems that the alleged shooter fired two shots, one hit Fireman White and the other hit the hood of his car. Both missed their intended target. Anyhow, I spoke to the magistrate and he told me that drive-by shootings were a federal offense in South Carolina. The shooter is looking at a forty to forty-five year sentence with no parole. That is the difference between federal time and state; you serve the entire sentence. As I am sure you will agree, it would be most appropriate for the alleged shooter to spend the rest of his natural life in prison.

I have already checked into PHIBGRU2 and will report every day until SHREVEPORT returns.

May the Lord bless and keep you all!

Very respectfully,
Chaplain Brown

From: CO@SHREVEPORT
To: CHAPS@NABLC
Re: Mission accomplished!

Chaps,

Great job with an incredibly difficult mission! Your compassion and understanding helped a family deal with a degree of grief I cannot begin to comprehend. You should be proud of your efforts.

The ship and crew are doing great, but working hard. We miss you and look forward to your return. We will be in Morehead City on 18 July 2001, so come on down if you can. Chief Ducass is doing a super job filling in for you during evening prayer. You have trained him well.

Again, you accomplished a great thing by being in South Carolina. I am sure even Fireman White had a smile on his face knowing that you were on scene taking care of his family.

R/CO

I prayed, by God's grace, that my efforts with the family did indeed make a difference. While I appreciated the captain's comments, I couldn't escape the fact that we had lost one of our best and brightest sailors.

-16-

JOINT TASK FORCE EXERCISE
Winding down on Work-Ups

30 July 2001

The Joint Task Force Exercise (JTFEX) was the culminating training evolution in preparation for our six-month deployment to the Mediterranean Sea. Ships, aircraft, assault vehicles, and landing crafts from the THEODORE ROOSEVELT Carrier Battle Group (TRBATGRU) and the BATAAN Amphibious Ready Group (BATARG) would essentially be spending twenty-one days at sea—between Norfolk and Puerto Rico—training to obtain their Ready-to-Deploy certification. It was our "bell lap" exercise before heading across the Atlantic Ocean.

The crew was beginning to feel the stress of the work-up cycle, spending at least half of a month during the past five months away from home. Even the ship, now over thirty years old, was showing its age. On our first day out of Norfolk, we experienced an engineering casualty in the Water Evaporator, or EVAP as it's known. With the EVAP down, water usage was severely restricted throughout the ship. If it remained this way for long, morale was going to take a big hit.

Letter to the AME Chaplain's Association

Dear Colleagues,

Praise God from whom all blessings flow!

It has been an exciting and challenging first year as your president. We have taken some positive strides towards achieving the goals that I set forth in my first correspondence last August. The "Chaplain's Corner" within the Church's newspaper has been revived and is up and running. Thus far, six articles from three separate chaplains have been published with many more anticipated to follow. Every article that is published brings glory to God and informs our Church of the diverse, dynamic ministry in which we serve.

Our first biannual Chaplain's Association Meeting held in Memphis, Tennessee was a rousing success on two fronts. First, it introduced our Bishop to the expansive parameters of responsibility he is entrusted with as the Ecclesiastical Endorsing Agent of the AME Church. Second, the notes from the conference recorded many bold and insightful suggestions and initiatives, some of which may become directives. On a personal note, I have endeavored to remain true to my pledge of staying in contact with you once a month and I will continue to do so.

The next hurdle I foresee is the compiling and editing of a body of by-laws. It is imperative that we have administrative guidelines to govern our association. I am planning to submit a rough draft throughout our association so that I can solicit input from you. It is important that everyone take the time to respond because once completed they will directly affect how we do business. I am projecting a deadline of October 2001 for a finished product. Here are professional and personal updates about some of our colleagues:

- Congratulations to Chaplain Roger Armstead on his promotion to Lieutenant Colonel! Chaplain Armstead serves at the Army Command and Staff College in Fort Leavenworth, Kansas.
- Congratulations to Chaplain Glenda Jennings Harrison, who completed her first deployment aboard the USS KITTY HAWK (CV-63)! Chaplain Jennings Harrison is stationed at the Naval Air Facility in Atsugi, Japan.

- Congratulations to Chaplain Charlotte Sydnor, who has received a pastoral appointment to Holly Grove AME Church in Windsor, Virginia.
- Godspeed to Chaplain Wilfred Bristol on his transition from his overseas assignment in Germany back to the United States.
- Chaplain Kenneth White, the most senior member of our association, deserves our prayers and merits our appreciation. He is a WWII and Korean War veteran who has served the Lord and his country faithfully. At age ninety-four, he traveled to the chaplain's conference in Memphis, Tennessee totally unassisted. Please pray for Chaplain White and contact him when you have the chance. You will find him to be a gracious sage, replete with a wisdom and clarity that belies his advanced years.
- Please take a moment to contact our brothers on "The Continent:" Chaplains James Fatuse and Daniel Kpodi of the South African Defense Force. A short note, card, or email offering your prayers and support will go a long way in letting them know that the multitude of miles separating us can never diminish their membership or our collegial connectivity.
- Welcome Aboard to our latest accession, LT Cassie Allen. Chaplain Allen is a Navy Chaplain from the Washington Annual Conference, Second Episcopal District who is currently stationed at the Marine Corps Recruit Depot in Parris Island, South Carolina.

In less than sixty days, I will begin my sojourn across the Atlantic Ocean to the Mediterranean Sea to execute a six-month deployment with my ship, the USS SHREVEPORT (LPD-12). This time shall be divided between shipboard preparations and quality time spent with my family. I ask for you to pray for the Lord's safety, protection, and strength to surround our family and our household as we prepare for this period of separation.
Until next month, may the Lord richly bless you all!

Sincerely,
LT David R. Brown
President, AME Chaplain's Association

This was the sixth letter to my fellow chaplains in AME and I was glad to get it out to them before I became too busy with my pastoral responsibilities aboard ship.

I was not supposed to be the president of the chaplain's association. It was not even my turn. You see, every four years the chaplains in the AME Church "elect" a new president at the AME General Conference. The presidency actually rotates between chaplains who serve the Armed Forces—Army, Navy, and Air Force—Veteran's Administration, and Federal Bureau of Prisons. Our tradition held that the senior chaplain within the rotation who is present at the conference is elected as President by consensus. Senior status was awarded by rank for the military; normally pay grades of O-5 or O-6, or by years of service for the Veteran's Administration and Bureau of Prisons.

In July of 2000, it was the Navy's turn in the rotation. The problem was that there were only three chaplains from the Navy who were present and all of us were lieutenants with a pay grade of 0-3. I was the senior of the three—my shipmates, chaplains Jennings Harrison and Buford were juniors respectively—so the lot fell on me to represent the Navy and, perhaps, the association. This was unsettling for my colleagues, so much so that they wanted to put it to an actual vote, nominating other senior chaplains to be placed on the ballot. Putting the wrong person in the president's position could have spelled disaster for our association, placing us in a politically vulnerable position in the Church.

While the president was preparing to organize our voting, candidates running for office came by our room to offer their "stump speech" because the election of bishops and general officers was scheduled to take place at the end of the week. The chaplain's association represented a block of thirty votes so the candidates had an interest in courting us. The president gladly welcomed a couple of candidates to come by and interrupt our business to campaign. However, when a female minister made the same request to address our association, the president who stated, "We did not have time right now to see any candidates", turned her away. I was hot! I knew what was going on and I did not like it at all. This minister was running for the office of Bishop in our church and any support she received could provide the edge she needed for election. However, the president was in charge of the meeting, no one was opposing him in his decision, and there was nothing that I could do about it.

God was watching and He had a plan. His ways are higher than ours.

The election took place by silent ballot. I was up against a senior military officer, whom by his sheer presence accentuated the fact that I was out-ranked and inexperienced. When it was all over, this was the tally: seventeen votes for me, fourteen votes for the other candidate—a near 50-50 split. I won but now I was the head of a house divided. The outgoing president invited me to the podium to address my colleagues. The tension in the room was thick as I began to speak. I noticed the mixed body language of the chaplains; some were supportive and paid attention, some stared down at the table before them or up at the ceiling above, noticeably disinterested in what I had to say. First, I thanked them all, told them how grateful I was to be their president, and I would work hard to gain their trust and confidence. I sensed that my words seemed like flowery, quixotic cloud cover to a group that wanted a substantive, focused, leadership statement.

Then suddenly, my blood pressure became elevated and I got very clear.

"Now, for my first order of business. Chaplain Buford, please go find the last minister who came by here and invite her to come back so she may address our group," I said.

"No problem!" Chaplain Buford said as he rose from his seat heading for the door.

"Oh! Make sure you tell her that the President of the AME Chaplain's Association personally invited her to come and speak to the chaplains. Make sure you tell her that!"

"You got it!" said Chaplain Buford as he departed.

I now had the attention of everyone in the room.

When she returned and addressed us, she spoke eloquently of her family's deep military lineage of service dating back to the Civil War. Later that week, she became the first woman to be elected and consecrated a bishop in the AME Church.

So that is how I became the president. I accepted the position even though I knew it was going to be a challenge. My experience as a naval officer trained me to thrive upon situations like this one. Besides, there were Army and Air Force officers present in the room that day and there was no way I was going to back out of a challenge like that right in front of them.

01 August

My supervisory chaplain at PHIBGRU2 wanted to receive weekly updates from all of his chaplains participating in the exercise. He had a reporting requirement with his CO that he had to fulfill. Of course, I was going to comply but I privately struggled with what or how much to report. I thought it best to provide a basic chronology from sunrise to sunset, submit it, and allow him to decide the salient points.

From: CHAPS@ SHREVEPORT
To: CHAPLAIN@PHIBGRU2
Subject: Weekly Update

Sir,

Here are my inputs for the weekly update:

29 JULY

- 0830: Inport Protestant Worship was held aboard ship. Six crewmembers were in attendance.

30 JULY

- 0615: Chaplain arrives aboard ship for JTFEX (30 JUL – 20 AUG)
- 0630: Officers' Call
- 0800: Underway from Pier 22
  Anchorage: Lynnhaven Inlet; embark Landing Craft Unit from NAB Little Creek
  Proceed south through moderate seas (five to seven feet) to Morehead City.
- 1500: Commence library and computer room renovations
- 2155: Evening Prayer at Sea

31 JULY

- 0500: Reveille
- 0530: Officers Call
- 0545: Sea and Anchor Detail; Condition 1-AIpha for Landing Craft Unit operations
- 0815: Moored at Morehead City
  Commence Anti-Terrorism/Force Protection Exercise
  Commence logistics onload
- 0930: Embark Marines from MSSG-26 and members of Seal Team 8
- 1130: Meet Chaplain McDowell (MSSG-26) for lunch.
- 1230: Daily Prayer Meeting–SACC
- 1500: Underway from Morehead City
- 1600: Shipboard reception for embarked personnel on the Signal Bridge.
  CO meets Chaplain McDowell; invited him to participate in Command Religious Program
- 1830: Eight o'clock Reports
- 2000: Bible Study (Mess Deck); sailors and Marines in attendance.
- 2145: Evening Prayer at Sea

01 AUGUST

- 0600: Reveille

- 0645: Officers Call
- 0800: Department Head Meeting
  Operations Officer (OPS) discussed deployment readiness issues
  OPS cited three areas of tasking for the Chaplain:
  Pre-deployment Report (NLT 20 AUG)
  Papal Audience Request-Rome (NLT 20 AUG)
  Project HANDCLASP and COMREL reports (during deployment)
- 0900: Man Overboard Drill
- Continue library and computer room renovations
  Hull Technicians (HTs) have the welding and cutting tasks
  Confirm computer delivery via Communications Officer (COMMO)

Still steaming south towards the Caribbean Operations Area. I will keep you informed concerning any other developments.

Very respectfully,
Chaplain Brown

My supervisor thanked me and offered no further comments or questions. So many things happen over the course of a day aboard ship. It is hard to capture what is important, or rather, what a supervisor would deem important. His silence in this instance was truly golden.

From: RB@HOME
To: CHAPS@SHREVEPORT
Subject: Nineteen days and counting...

Good morning!

Our son has been sitting on my lap while I am trying to type this message saying "Dadda." He wants to type. Here is his message.

tgfgfdcfdcidds a,;jkkkkkkkkkkkkkkkkm sij hrjdjkfogsfsdd u ibkckcfvksxuxcx j

We will try to get out of the house sometime today to get some air. All is well at the homestead. Please keep prayed-up.

5THINGS

God's continued presence in my life
How God sustains us when we are tired
God's peace that passes understanding
Our son's growth
Our family

Love,
RB

From: CHAPS@SHREVEPORT
To: RB@HOME
Re: Nineteen days and counting...

Hey!

Give our son a hug for his very first email! :-)

We are almost finished in Morehead City and then it is back out to sea. I have met the chaplain serving with the Marine unit aboard ship, Chaplain McDowell. I met him for lunch today in the Wardroom and he seems like an easy-going guy. Later, he came to the Daily Prayer Meeting and he will probably show up for Bible Study tonight.

The exciting event for today was: a steam pipe burst in our office and spewed steam for at least fifteen minutes before someone reported it to Damage Control Central. The spray of steam cooled and condensed into water, which covered the floor to about a half-inch depth. Nothing electrical was damaged but it made a soggy mess of any cardboard and paper items on the floor. The flood was discovered at 1245 and it was all cleaned up by 1430. It has not interrupted my schedule too much, though. I have been using another computer up in the admin department to get my work done. This *old* ship!

We have begun to renovate the computer room and library spaces. RP1 Bates and I spent part of the morning taking down the books and their racks and relocating them to a storage room. We should have all the work completed by the time we pull into Norfolk.

Stay strong in the Lord and the strength of His might. I will keep praying on this end and will continue to stay in touch.

Love,
Chaps

"TATTOO, TATTOO! LIGHTS OUT IN FIVE MINUTES! STAND BY FOR THE EVENING PRAYER."

Steadfast Consistency of the Lord

Let us pray.

Gracious Lord, we give praise to you because you are
unchanging in all your ways.
You protect our lives in spite of the risks we accept, the sacrifices we make, and
the Service for which we signed up. You watch over our loved ones who are
far beyond our reach and our control. You comfort us in our distress through
valleys so low, so private, and so solitary.

In our profession where so much is planned,
we can never rule out Murphy's Law.

In a world where promises are so easily made but not always as easily kept,
trust is a rare commodity.

Lord, our encouragement arises from the knowledge that You never change.
Dependable as the sunrise, your mercy is new every day.
Consistent as the swell of the tides, your love is everlasting.
Certain as the saltiness of the sea, you are completely faithful.

Continue to steam south with us monitoring our lives as every f
orgotten mile sweeps beneath the keel.
Provide a wide berth for safe passage as abundant and clear
as the surrounding horizon.
Love us deeply: deeper than the indigo depths could ever hope to reach.

Amen.

02 August
From: CHAPS@SHREVEPORT
To: RB@HOME
Subject: Water hours

Hey!

We are out of water out here. I know that sounds funny but our Water Evaporator went down for several hours a couple of days ago and the ship has imposed a water usage restriction ever since. They think the cause was excessive usage—53,000 gallons or three times above normal. Even though they have fixed the EVAP, the ship is so far behind it cannot keep up with the demand. The safe percentage of water aboard ship is above 85 percent capacity. This morning it was at 45 percent, hence, the water restriction. I am doing well otherwise. I did get my shower and it is going to have to hold me until 0600 tomorrow morning. Can you believe it? They literally shut off the water so you cannot even take a shower. I spoke to the Chief Engineer and he said the only way we will get back above 85 percent is to pull into Roosevelt Roads, Puerto Rico and spend three days replenishing the tanks. Just another test for SHREVEPORT!

5THINGS

God's power and presence
His ability to sustain us through whatever
Our family
Our relationship
Seventeen days and counting

I will be lifting you both up in prayer. I have already claimed peace for you and our son this afternoon.

Take care,
Chaps

Encouraged

Let us pray.

*Gracious Lord, there are many ways for us to stay encouraged
and motivated while at sea.*

Some ways are connected to our vocation:

*Knowing our service and sacrifice counts for something
Unit cohesion—the ability to belong to something greater than yourself
Mission accomplishment and Esprit de Corps*

Some ways are more practical:

Glancing at photos of loved ones in picture frames or taped to bulkheads
A headset and a CD player with the volume on high
Anticipating a return email message
A good round of PT to pass the time

Still, other ways are more idealistic:

Daydreams drifting like a kite without a tether
That feeling of euphoria that follows coming off of Watch
Seventeen days and counting

Lord, nothing can compare to the encouragement you provide.
First, just your presence alone is enough to lift our spirit; you set things
in order and help us to hold our peace. You drive away our worries and
supplement our shortcomings. You grant us victory over the "Goliath"
situations in our lives. We are the grateful recipients of your love and
forgiveness.

Then, you have given us each other. We serve together for much more than the
execution of our orders; we are here for mutual support, to be there for each
other in crisis or calm. We are responsible and you hold us accountable. You
have placed us here to stand in the gap, go the extra mile, to build each other
up, and not tear down.
Thank you, Lord, for all they ways we stay encouraged at sea and most
importantly the ultimate encouragement that you provide.

Amen.

"TAPS, TAPS, LIGHTS OUT! ALL HANDS TURN TO YOUR BUNKS.
MAINTAIN SILENCE ABOUT THE DECKS. TAPS!"

03 August
From: CHAPS@SHREVEPORT
To: RB@HOME
Re: Water hours

Well, we are still struggling through water hours and to top it off, the washer machine broke down. Oh! I forgot to bring my Summer White uniform for manning the rail. I will just hang back out of sight when the ship pulls into Puerto Rico.

I am still compiling my evening prayers and notes for "Spirit Soundings." The most challenging thing so far is getting the prayers in proper order, especially my earliest ones. When I came to SHREVEPORT, I wrote my prayers in magic marker and never dated them. However, I always laid them one-on-top-of-the-other in chronological order. I have found a couple of key prayers like the night after I did the burials at sea. I try to pinpoint that date and count up or down based on the length of days we were at sea. The prayers from last November have been the most challenging to track but I am doing my best to get them straight.

Have a blessed and peaceful evening and I will talk to you tomorrow.

Love,
Chaps

A Long Day at Sea

Let us pray.

Gracious Lord, we have had a long day at sea to simply do what we do as sailors and Marines. It has been good to spread our wings so to speak; to train personnel and dry run equipment to expose the kinks and glitches.

SHREVEPORT is stretching her muscles to warm up for the half-year marathon overseas.

Lord, what we do is never really simple at all. If it was, anyone could do it. Furthermore, one must not only do it well but also be the best. It is what our nation requires and the free world deserves. Hence, the late hours, the overnight Boat and Anchor Crane operations, the "0-Dark-30" pack-out of Marines going ashore—it is all part of the process of keeping the spearhead sharp. The demands are grueling. Yet, we cannot afford to not pay attention to our work because the probable cost incurred would be too great.

So, quite simply, we petition you tonight. Lord, continue to keep us strong, safe, smart, vigilant, focused—all of the above—so that we may reap and store the benefits of this long day at sea.

We ask this in your Mighty Name,
Amen.

05 August

The Test

Let us pray.

Gracious Lord, our hearts are thankful tonight because our training has gone so well thus far. You have allowed us to employ the best of our skill and experience to execute the evolutions that comprise JTFEX.

We would like to say that it has been easy; but it has not.
We would like to say that things have run smoothly; but they have not.
We would like to say that things have gone our way; sometimes they have, other times not, but-all-in-all we have managed to be successful.

Our business is a test. It is inseparable from what we do; like yeast lost in the dough allowing it to rise and become something that it could never be on its own.

Our work is a challenge. It pushes and pulls, stretches and constrains, fatigues and exhilarates, frustrates and satisfies; it pounds on us like a blacksmith's hammer striking hot glowing iron.

Our service is designed to bring out the best in us—and it has, and it does, and it will.

Thank you, Lord, for our tests; thank you that you are our God over them, our God in them, and our God through them.

Amen.

07 August
From: CHAPS@SHREVEPORT
To: RB@HOME
Subject: Thirteen days and counting

Hey!

Today is welding day for the new computer room. The HTs (welders) have to measure and cut some plate steel in order to make the tables for the new computers. Hopefully, they will be finished by Friday so we can come back and paint, put in electrical sockets, and Internet cable next week.

Chaplain McDowell is a huge help in ministry! We have set a schedule for the evening prayer. I have Mondays, Wednesdays, Fridays, and Sundays. He has the other three days. This is contingent upon him being on ship because there will be times when he must go ashore with his Marines. That means we need to keep close tabs on our daily schedules.

5THINGS

Another day to serve the Lord
Being one day closer to you
The ministry aboard ship
Our son's growth and development
Our family

Ensign Luckie has extended an invitation for dinner at his house. He thought that 24 August would be a good date. I have not responded because I wanted to see what you thought about it. Think it over and respond when you are ready.

We are having an ice cream social tonight on the Mess Deck at 2000. They are hoping it will offset the "missing" water and boost morale before pulling into Puerto Rico.

I AM PRAYING TODAY...

for God's continued grace, strength, and protection over your lives.
for an "enlarged territory" in ministry.
for safe training evolutions.
for a safe return home.

Have a blessed day!

Love,
Chaps

From: RB@HOME
To: CHAPS@SHREVEPORT
Re: Thirteen days and counting

What a morning! I decided to cut the lawn. The ninety plus degree temperature and heat index of 105 did not help. The job is done and I will not have to face it again before you get back.

The 24th of August sounds good. I have nothing on the calendar for that day. Please find out what we should bring.

5THINGS

God allowing me to see one more day
God's continued blessings in my life
God providing strength for me to finish the lawn
A God that answers prayers
A loving family
Continue to pray for our family.

Love,
RB

08 August
"REVEILLE, REVEILLE! ALL HANDS HEAVE OUT! BREAKFAST FOR THE CREW!"

From: CHAPS@SHREVEPORT
To: RB@HOME
Subject: Pulling into Roosevelt Roads

Good morning!

We are turning the corner on Vieques and heading slightly south to Roosevelt Roads for a 0900 mooring at the pier. The captain has granted Liberty today until 2200, just as I suspected. He announced that there would be an MWR Shuttle to take us onto the main part of the base. The first thing I am going to find is a laundry mat. Three days of waiting on parts for our broken washer machine has piled the clothes up to the limit. I am glad that I brought that extra underwear from home because it helped me to hold out. Thank you, Lord!

The ice cream social was sort of a bust. They gave us a choice of flavors: chocolate chip, strawberry, or butter pecan. It was definitely not Breyers but it served its purpose. We could have it in a cone or a cup and as much as we wanted. It was not a social at all; it was more of a "get your ice cream and go" kind of gathering. I had the butter pecan. Please have some of the real stuff on hand when I get home.

5THINGS

The Lord in my life
The way the Lord encourages me
The way you encourage me just by hearing your voice :-)
Our terrific family
Twelve days and counting...

5PRAYERS

I am praying for your strength in the Lord today.
I am praying for our son.
I am praying for access to washer machines and dryers.
I am praying for more ministry aboard the ship.
I am praying for safe travel for you this weekend.
I will give you a call when I come into port. Stay encouraged! Read Psalm 24 to be reminded of the Lord's strength.

Love,
Chaps

09 August
In Port: Puerto Rico
From: CHAPS@SHREVEPORT
To: RB@HOME

Hey!

The island is pretty much the same as we left it back in April, except not as green. It seems that summer is not the rainy season around here. When we were here last everything was so much more plush and vivid in their hues; more flowers were blossoming too. Still, it is very scenic, warm, breezy, and humid.

I enjoyed talking to you on the phone yesterday. The more I hear you the more encouraged I become. I praise God for the way he is blessing and keeping you within his care in spite of the lost hours of sleep. Somehow, someway he blesses you with strength and soundness of mind for another day. Thank you, Lord!

Chaplain Buford picked me up at the ship at 1800 last evening for dinner. He and his wife live over in an area called Bundy Housing. The entire complex is located on a small isthmus that is dotted with Caribbean pastel-colored ranch homes. Each one is individual, made of concrete, and is about the same square footage. Their home is light turquoise on the outside and all white on the inside. We sat and talked for a few hours over a "down home" meal. His wife works with him at the hospital so every morning they go to work together. They would like to be stationed in the States next, perhaps Camp Pendleton, California. I told them if they get it they have got to go to three places: San Diego, the Souplantation restaurant, and Las Vegas. Just thinking about those three makes me want to get some reservations. :-)

No word yet if we will get Liberty today or not but I will give you a call either way.

5THINGS

Our strong relationship with the Lord
Our strong relationship with each other
Our beautiful, growing son
Safe passage and mooring in Puerto Rico
Ten days and counting
Take care and have a blessed day.

Love,
Chaps

From: CHAPS@SHREVEPORT
To: CHAPLAIN@PHIBGRU2
Subject: Weekly Update (09 AUG)

Sir,

Everything is going very well here at Roosevelt Roads. WHIDBEY ISLAND
and BATAAN are moored to our port and will be until we depart tomorrow.
Here are the inputs for the weekly update:

03 AUGUST
- BATAAN ARG arrived in vicinity of Vieques.
- 0830: Two small speedboats greeted our ship, about 1500 yards off
  of our port bow. Our GMs were given the order to man the gun
  mounts and they did. I think the two boats got close enough to see
  the Fifty Cals pointed at them so they kept on going, passing parallel to the ship.
- 1230: Daily Prayer Meeting (SACC)
- LMRC renovations continue. HTs measured and cut the steel that
  will become the tabletops for the new computers.
- Chaplain McDowell gave his first Evening Prayer at Sea.

04 AUGUST

- 0100: Seventeen CRCCs speedboats launched, carrying Marines from Lima Company (3/6). They continued small boat operations throughout the day.
- Chaplain McDowell hopped a ride on one of the CRCCs, spent all day ashore; returned sunburned and sore but okay.
- 1230: Daily Prayer Meeting (SACC)
- Worship preparations were made for a joint Protestant service. I led the liturgy and Chaplain McDowell preached.
- Received email from Chaplain Hogan from BATAAN. He is trying to arrange flight ops to come over and conduct Roman Catholic Mass. He conceded that things would be more hopeful during the latter part of JTFEX.

05 AUGUST

- 0400: SHREVEPORT departed Vieques OP AREA to conduct a C-WIS shoot. The Fire Controlmen successfully shot down two drones.
- 0900: Protestant Divine Services. Thirty sailors and Marines attended.
- SHREVEPORT headed back to Vieques OP AREA to rejoin BATAAN ARG.

06 AUGUST

- CRRC Operations continued
- While conducting deckplate visit to Main Control, I discovered that the Evaporator was down again. It stayed that way for several hours. Overall affect: reduction of percentage of freshwater, which led to more "water hours."
- 1230: Daily Prayer Meeting (SACC)
- Contacted the Fleet and Family Support Center, Ombudsman, and Spouse Support Group concerning Parent/Child Pre-deployment brief on 13 September at 1900 aboard SHREVEPORT.
- Chaplain McDowell conducted evening prayer.

07 AUGUST

- Last day of Strategic Arms Exercise (SACEX) and "Gator Zigzags" along the coast of Vieques.
- CNET responded to our request for new computers to support the Library Media Resource Center (LMRC).
- 1230: Daily Prayer Meeting (SACC)
- 1900: NAVOPS INTEL Brief: Our transit into Roosevelt Roads was briefed.

08 AUGUST

- 0130: HTs commence work on installing tabletops. Work completed by 0500. After replacing some lagging, the tabletops along with the bulkheads will receive a fresh coat of paint (white for bulkheads, haze gray for tables).
- 0800: Around Vieuques for short transit into Roosevelt Roads. Embark Harbor pilots with special guest: Chaplain Bezy, an Episcopal Priest attached to the Caribbean Crossroads Chapel at Roosevelt Roads. Chaplain Bezy had greeting tables and an ice chest filled with sodas at each pier for the ships of BATAAN ARG. Religious literature covered each table along with the schedules of the Sunday worship services. He was not informed that we would be departing before the weekend. A smart move in ministry on his part, though.
- 0900: Moored. SHREVEPORT commenced her Anti-Terrorism/ Force Protection Exercise—shipboard and pier side.

Very respectfully,
Chaplain Brown

10 August
Underway: Puerto Rico
From: CHAPS@SHREVEPORT
To: RB@HOME

Hey!

We are leaving Roosevelt Roads this morning. It has being called a hostile breakaway because the final action of our exercise will be to leave the port with "terrorists" trying to block our way. Once we clear, we will make a left turn and head north as quickly as possible.

I had another good evening with Chaplain Buford. He asked me to lead his Bible Study at the chapel. It was a good group of eight people, who were quieter than I am used to. Perhaps they were not used to my style of teaching. Following study, I went over his house for dinner and then returned to the ship. The Buford's hospitality made this "working port" a bit more pleasant.

I miss you terribly. When you get tired, I wish I were there to be your support. I know that the Lord is sustaining you but my feelings remain the same.

5THINGS

Another day to serve the Lord
Another day closer to you
The hospitality of the Bufords
Our son
The "expanding territory" aboard ship

Have a safe, blessed trip today to Richmond. I will continue to email while you are there. Please tell everybody that I said, "Hello."

Love,
Chaps

From: RB@HOME
To: CHAPS@SHREVEPORT

I am glad you had another good evening. We did too! Thank you for the phone call this morning.

We are getting ready for our trip to Richmond today. Mom is taking some time off to be with us. It should be good.

One thing I forgot to ask is what days do you have off in September? I have to schedule an appointment and I do not want it to interfere with a workday. Please let me know when you can.

5THINGS

God's continued care over our household and family
The blood of Jesus, which protects us from hurt, harm, or danger
Your love and thoughtfulness
Our son
Nine more days and counting

Take care and have a blessed trip to Morehead City!

Love,
RB

14 August
From: RB@HOME
To: CHAPS@SHREVEPORT
Subject: Good morning

Hi Chaps!

How are you? We are doing fine. We had a good day here and I think we will stick around Richmond for another few days then head home. This visit has been a good and nice break. We both have been getting more sleep here than at home, funny, but I hope that trend continues. :-)

5THINGS

The way God's word picks me up when I am feeling down
Mom and Dad and their love and generosity
Our son
A good night's sleep
The way God is richly blessing our family

I hope all is well with you and the crew. Take care and I hope to talk to you soon.

Love,
RB

15 August
From: CHAPS@SHREVEPORT
To: CHAPLAIN@ PHIBGRU2
Subject: Weekly Update (15 AUG)

Sir,

Here are the updates from last week:

09 AUGUST
- ATFP exercise continued. The ship goes from condition BRAVO to CHARLIE, effectively securing liberty for most of the day. During this time, there were "protestors", swimmers, and boaters who

"threatened" the ship's security. All efforts to compromise security were thwarted.

- 1700: Met with Chaplain Maurice Buford, Command Chaplain at the Naval Hospital in Roosevelt Roads. Chaplain Buford invited me to lead his 1800 Bible Study at the Caribbean Crossroads Chapel, to, which I obliged.
- 0000: Ship goes the condition "Delta:" Liberty secured, pier secured, RHIB and SBU boats run round the clock waterborne patrols.

10 AUGUST

- 0800: SBU and RHIB boats escorted Underway-Ship out of the harbor. CDR Crow (COMPHIBGRU2 ATFP Evaluator) was embarked.
- 1000: SHREVEPORT turns northwest (320) and heads for Onslow Bay area.
- 1230: Daily Prayer meeting
- LMRC electrical wiring began
- Contacted PHIBROON 8 Chaplain to coordinate Holy HELO flight to bring Chaplain Hogan over from BATAAN.
- 2155: Evening Prayer at sea

11 AUGUST

- Steel Beach Picnic planned for 1500-1700
- 1440: Chaplain Hogan arrived from BATAAN via Holy HELO. He conducted a 1530 Mass with 15 participants and counseled with Catholic Lay Reader, Lt. j.g. Depke.
- All hands on the Flight Deck for Steel Beach Picnic
- 1830: Chaplain Hogan departed for BATAAN.
- 2155: Evening Prayer conducted by Chaplain McDowell (MSSG-26)

12 AUGUST

- 0900: Divine Protestant Service. Chaplain McDowell was worship leader while I preached; twenty-nine Marines and sailors in attendance.
- 1230: Daily Prayer Meeting
- Continue north-northwest transit towards Onslow Bay OP AREA
- 2155: Evening Prayer at Sea.

13 AUGUST

- Painting commenced in LMRC.
- First JTFEX tasks were received from PHIBRON 8. Specific ships and subs from the TRBATGRU were designated as hostile. Possible Non-Combatant Evacuation (NEO), Mass Casualty exercise will be conducted.
- OPSECCON 1 was set throughout the ship. Email and POTS line phone calls are restricted until further notice.
- 1230: Daily Prayer Meeting.
- Minefield simulation: Swept Channel transit for BATAAN ARG. TRBATGRU ships (Destroyers and Cruiser escorting).
- 2155: Evening Prayer at Sea

14 AUGUST

- OPSECON 1 still set throughout the ship.
- Swept Channel transit to 150 miles off the coast of North Carolina concluded.
- LMRC painting concluded
- 2000: Bible study, Mess Deck

15 AUGUST

- Red Cross message: Report of Death of loco parentis father. Service member will take LCU ashore then take Leave to include POM period.

- LCU Operations ashore. Marines (MSSG-26) headed to the beach to set up base camp fifty miles inland.
- LMRC was wired for LAN connections by ITs. Computers still scheduled to arrive 22 August 2001.

We are still doing "Gator Zigzags" off the beach and will do so until the end of the exercise. It has been a long underway but God is good—all the time—and we will be home soon.

Take care and God bless you!

Very respectfully,
Chaplain Brown

I tried to put the best spin on this week's report, making it sound as positive and upbeat as I could. I had been spending so much time watching out for the needs of the crew that I was not paying attention to myself. The cumulative effect of boundless pastoral care—constant ministry of presence about the ship, often at odd and early hours, numerous counseling appointments, expanding administrative tasks and responsibilities, and being strong for everyone—began to take its toll. I did not want to tell him that I was worn out and emotionally flat.

"TATTOO, TATTOO! LIGHTS OUT IN FIVE MINUTES! STAND BY FOR THE EVENING PRAYER."

The Test Continues

Gracious Lord,

We find ourselves fully immersed into JTFEX having to execute each new tasking we receive. And so, our test continues.

In tactics, the vast reserve of our ability and experience is on the line.

Motivate us, Lord, to react to every changing scenario.
As colleagues, our bond of interdependence is being bent and checked for stress
fractures. Help us, Lord, to maintain our composure and mutual respect.

Through time, we seek to count down the remaining days at sea. Yet, too
much effort may jeopardize our focus. Thank you, Lord, for the work
that does not give our attention span a break and allows one day to fold
into the next.

Lord, our work continually inquires of us, "How long? How often? How
much? and How far?" Our response is always, "Whatever it takes."

We are finite creatures, though, and our energy and enthusiasm wane even to
the point where we sometimes simply run out of gas. So we need you tonight
to stoke the fires of our endurance, stir up the glowing embers of our willpower,
and fan into the flame of our vigilance so that fatigue and lethargy do
not douse the blaze within. Our desire is to exercise the capabilities you
have given us.

This we pray in your Mighty Name,
Amen.

16 August
About Noon

I sat in my stateroom staring at my desk, exhausted with nothing left to give. I had no devotion prepared for the prayer meeting and I found it difficult to get motivated to put something together. I finally decided just to be honest with the men about how I felt.

"DAILY PRAYER MEETING WILL BE HELD IN SACC AT 1230."

Help me to be honest with my brothers, Lord, and to ask for their prayers.

I left my stateroom with no pride to swallow, Bible in hand, but seeming more as a token of my position on the ship rather than anything else.

Just after 1600
From: CHAPS@SHREVEPORT
To: DAILYPRAYER@SHREVEPORT
Subject: REFRESHED AND BLESSED!

Brothers!

What a blessed time I had at the Daily Prayer Meeting! I was out of gas due to my early mornings and exhausting nights. I knew that I had to get together with you for prayer but my mind and body wanted some "rack time." Well, the presence and power of the Holy Spirit—through you—provided "the wind beneath my wings." I left the meeting lifted, just as if I had ten hours of sleep! I felt so good that I left our meeting and went to the gym for a half hour. Praise God for men like you who believe in our prayer-answering God!

Thanks again for lifting me today!

Yours in Christ,
Chaplain Brown

Fellow Christians from the Daily Prayer Meeting

From: YN1BROWN@SHREVEPORT
To: CHAPS@SHREVEPORT
Re: BLESSED AND REFRESHED!

Praise God! Something about our daily prayer meeting that I cannot explain. God is good all the time.

V/r
YN1 (SW) Brown

From: PC2TRAMMEL@SHREVEPORT
To: CHAPS@SHREVEPORT
Re: BLESSED AND REFRESHED!

Brother, you are so welcome. I am rejoicing too! God did not bring you this far to leave you.

V/r,
PC2 Trammel

I received several other messages like these from the other sailors who were at the prayer meeting. I began to realize that this group of men was in my life not just so I could provide for their spiritual needs. They walked with and strengthened me through this ministry experience. The Lord blessed me with a solid core of Christians to surround, support, and encourage me.

17 August
From: CHAPS@SHREVEPORT
To: RB@HOME
Subject: Good morning!

Hey!

Today, as I suspected, will be busier than yesterday, which will help the time go by faster. We are down to two and a half days left! I remember when there were twenty days left. Once again, our God is carrying us all the way. "Through many dangers, toils, and snares..." he is watching over us and providing for our needs.

The First Lieutenant is taking his family to see his relative in New York. He is going to stay at Fort Hamilton, an old Army base located directly under the Verazzano Narrows Bridge. He did not have the number to the lodging office, though. I was wondering if you could look it up in the military lodging book and send it to me so I may forward it to him. Also, if you have some time today, call the Coast Guard station in Buxton, North Carolina to reconfirm our reservations. I secured it under "LT Brown." That number is taped to the fridge.

Funny thing: The 1MC started to break up again just as I was doing the evening prayer, causing the ship to hear excerpts of the prayer separated by unexpected moments of silence. About two seconds after I finished, the captain's "hotline" rang in the Pilot House. Well, he was hot! He told the Officer-of-the-Deck to "Fix that @#%+ 1MC 'cause we can't hear the chaplain pray!"

The Internal Communication (IC) Sailor on Watch was summoned to the Pilot House to fix the problem. This was the second time this happened this week and I guess the captain was fed up. I am encouraged that he listens and wants everyone else to hear too. Tonight before I pray, I am going to have the Boatswain Mate-of-the-Watch do a microphone test to ensure it is working properly.

5THINGS

Our family
Our love and our relationship
Our son's development
For the blessing of knowing Jesus
Two and a half days and counting

Write back when you can.

Love,
Chaps

2145
Pilot House

"Officer-of-the-Deck," called the Boatswain Mate through the darkness.
"Officer-of-the-Deck, Aye!" he responded.
"Request a Short Count Test of the 1MC from the Pilot House," he said.
"Very well," said the OOD.
Boats picked up the 1MC, keyed the microphone, and announced:
"The following is a Short Count Test of the 1MC from the Pilot House: 1-2-3, 3-2-1; test complete."
"'Sounds like it is working, Boats," I said.
"Yes, Sir. It does. You should be good-to-go," he said.
I was going to be good-to-go whether it worked or not but I slightly pitied those on Watch in the Pilot House if it did not, particularly the OOD

and Boatswain Mate-of-the-Watch. The captain was going to have some-one's head if it failed.

"Officer-of-the-Deck," called Boats.

"O-O-D, Aye!"

"Tattoo?" he requested.

"Very well," the OOD replied.

"'Ready Chaps?" he asked.

"'Ready Boats."

"TATTOO, TATTOO! LIGHTS OUT IN FIVE MINUTES! STAND BY FOR THE EVENING PRAYER."

Stay Encouraged (ENDEX)

Let us pray.

Gracious Lord, the end of our exercise is approaching and you have blessed us all along the way. As the final waves of Marines go ashore, as we meander back and forth along the coastline, we cannot help but feel encouraged tonight.

We can see the light at the end of the tunnel: the checkered flag is being unfurled and we can envision a crowd of supporters gathering to meet us at the Pier 5 finish Line.

Before our attention turns north, running a track fluent with the Gulf Stream and parallel to the Outer Banks, we have a need to stay encouraged and focused all at the same time.
This can be a tall task because encouragement is sometimes a breeding ground for euphoria, which can blur our focus and allow it to slip away like a ship that has lost steerage due to contrary winds and seas. Lord, while going home is a good thing, taking care of business—safely and intelligently—will make homecoming that much more sweet.

So Lord, keep us encouraged, having you as our heart's delight, and homecoming as the fruition of our desire. Keep us focused on your presence, on our work, our mission, and our shipmates.

All this we pray in your Holy Name,
Amen.

We all paused for a moment, waiting to see if the captain's hotline would ring. About thirty seconds passed—nothing but silence.

"Okay, Boats. Looks like we are good-to-go," I said.

"Yes, Sir. No calls. That is a good thing," he said.

"Good night, Boats."

"Good night, Chaps."

19 August

This morning, the captain came over the 1MC and announced to the crew that we had been released early from JTFEX. We were cleared to go home. All day long the euphoria felt and expressed about the ship was as tangible as it was contagious. Much of the laughter and conversation focused on these questions: "What are you doing? Where are you going for the Standown Leave period?" Each Sailor aboard the ship was guaranteed fifteen days off once we returned to Norfolk. Leave would be granted on a "Port" and "Starboard" basis, that is, half of the crew would be on Leave during the first fifteen days, the other half during the second. With the deployment exactly one month away, it was a sure bet that everyone had some sort of plan for vacation.

Unexpected Blessings

Let us pray.

Gracious Lord, we praise you tonight for being released from our tasking so that we could return home a day early. We are fortunate to be the recipients of this unexpected blessing.

Lord, if you bestowed your favor based upon merit, we would have good cause to expect to be blessed by your hand. For during this underway period, we have worked tirelessly, trained vigorously, and endured hardship patiently. If there was ever a crew that deserved a break, it is our own.

However, it is good to know that your favor is not based upon merit but emanates from your loving nature, which blesses us even when we do not deserve it. In fact, it is those times when we are less than deserving that we still come to you and ask for your favor and blessing.

Thank you, Lord, for all of your unexpected blessings. Keep each member of the crew and their loved ones safe during the Standown Leave periods. This we pray in your Blessed Name, Amen.

"TAPS, TAPS, LIGHTS OUT! ALL HANDS TURN TO YOUR BUNKS. MAINTAIN SILENCE ABOUT THE DECKS. TAPS!"

CAPE HATTERAS
Sanctuary by the sea

I am not certain if the American artist Andrew Wyeth ever visited the Outer Banks of North Carolina. Much of its landscape strongly resembles subject matter that he would have painted; especially during overcast days when the solitary wetlands and wildlife preserves that border the Pamlico Sound took on an austere and unspoiled quality. Cape Hatteras was a sanctuary, a seashore asylum from the pace and priorities of daily life.

Most who visit the Outer Banks for the first time usually travel some distance—four to six hours—and they first encounter the very pleasant towns of Kitty Hawk and Nags Head and go no further down the island. These towns, though, are much like Virginia Beach, Virginia or Ocean City, Maryland or Wildwood, New Jersey or Coney Island, New York—commercial, exciting, convenient. I much preferred all the territory below the *Cape Hatteras National Seashore* sign on Highway 12 South. There I could be off the RADAR Screen and disappear for a while, which was very appealing to me after a ten months of arduous sea duty.

Hatteras Island was a thin ribbon of sand, less than a mile wide in some spots, positioned south-southeast that jutted out into the Gulf Stream. I had been coming to the island since I was a teenager. Growing up in New Jersey spoiled me because it had its own beach culture, "Down the Shore", most of which I could enjoy in less than an hour's drive. Its ease and accessibility made me believe that the Jersey Shore was the only beach I would ever need. However, that all changed during the summer of my fifteenth year when my grandparents invited my family down to the Cape. Until then, I had never known a beach without a boardwalk or having to be careful not to step on stretched-out sunbathers on my way to the water.

Our trip down to the Outer Banks was short, just over two-and-a-half hours from Chesapeake, Virginia down to our destination in the town of Buxton. The U.S. Coast Guard had a station adjacent to the Cape Hatteras Lighthouse. We had reservations at the recreational lodging facility on the station and at sixty-five bucks-a-night, it was a steal. We had the best vacation plan too, the kind with no agenda. Well, perhaps some agenda: lots of sun, surf, sand, and sleep.

It was just us three—wife, toddler son in the back seat, and me—heading down Highway 12 South, a two-lane highway all the way down the entire length of Hatteras Island. Once we left civilization and entered the national seashore, I knew we had just about an hour left on our journey exhibiting the most scenic part of the trip. The Bodie Island Lighthouse sat about a mile back from the road with its black and white stripped parallel-lined design. The Oregon Inlet housed a charter fishing marina and Coast Guard Station Annex. The Herbert C. Bonner Bridge, which spanned over the inlet, began at sea level but rose several hundred feet high to accommodate the largest fishing vessels offered spectacular views—fifteen miles in every direction—on a clear day. Pea Island Wildlife Refuge contained sprawling marshlands extending into the Pamlico Sound and was home to native and migratory bird species. We slowed our speed to thirty-five miles-per-hour once we reached the villages of Salvo, Rodanthe, and Waves. We increased our speed back up to fifty-five miles-per-hour for fourteen more miles of solitary highway with dense brush vegetation and beach and Sound access points on each side. Finally, we reached Avon, the last well-developed village before Buxton.

As we drove through Avon, my wife began to notice a neighborhood with scores of luxury vacation properties.

"Wow! Look at those houses over there," my wife exclaimed looking to her right.

"Yeah, that is Kinnakeet Shores. It is the 'High Rent District,'" I said.

"Those homes are beautiful," she said.

"Yeah, but we will never be able to afford anything over there. The homes must go for five to six hundred thousand a piece," I said.

"How is he doing back there?" I asked inquiring about our son.

"He is asleep," she half-whispered.

"Great! We only have a few more miles until we reach the Coast Guard Station," I said.

We departed Avon and onto the last solitary stretch of highway. Almost immediately, we could spot Buxton—six miles away—due to the town's most prominent feature, the Cape Hatteras Lighthouse. Its black and white diagonal swirl-stripped design could be discerned even from that distance and it is the tallest lighthouse in America. This stretch of road would serve as my morning running route and I was hoping to get in about forty miles before our vacation was done. We finally made it to Buxton where my Hatteras Island experiences began nearly twenty-one years ago.

"Do you know where we turn for the Coast Guard Station?" asked my wife.

"Yeah. It is a left turn at the Red Drum Tackle Shop. The station should be at the end of the street," I said.

We made that turn and headed down the street. The old Hodges Motel was still there on the left—even the outdoor fish cleaning tables, where my father, brothers and I prepared many Spots and Pompanos for dinner. We slowed to a stop once we arrived at the front gate and I showed the petty officer on guard my Active Duty ID card. He permitted us aboard the station. The lodging facility check-in was the first turn on our right, around the circle, and down the road. I parked the car and went to the front desk to get the room key. We had reserved the Queen Suite. With room for four people, it was more space than we needed but we were glad to have it just to stretch out a bit. The air conditioner was already on and the room was refreshingly cool. We made it!

Morning Run

I got up about 5:00 a.m. so I could go running. My route was north on Highway 12 up to Avon and back in time for "wake up" and breakfast with my family. I got dressed in some PT gear, had a short prayer, grabbed my ID, room key, and a couple of dollars, and left the room. Once I stepped outside it was still dark, the only illumination was from some of the street-lights on the station and the ambient light from the town. The light from the lighthouse was still spinning and I was close enough to it to see the dual, bi-lateral, rotating beam of light. At this close distance, I could actually see the beam projecting out over the ocean. From a distance ten miles or further, its light was only discernible as blink or a flicker.

I did some stretching to warm up and get the blood pumping. I began running slowly to warm up as I went, but also to be careful of the hazards hidden in the darkness. Things like small potholes, stones, and uneven pavement, could make me trip and fall or twist an ankle. There would be several miles of the trip where the darkness would hide all of these, which was part of the reason I prayed before I left.

There was a point to the morning run to Avon—more than simply running for time or distance covered. It was *me time*: a personal space for peace and quiet devotions, prayer, therapy, and counseling all at the same time. Only the Lord, the skies, the sea, the Sound, and the roads were present. It was two hours of uninterrupted decompression. I had to be careful, though, for the occasional car or truck that would be on the road at that time of the morning. Since I always ran into traffic—north on the southbound lane, then vice versa—the hazard was increased. It was not so much that the vehicle was going to hit me, but its lights would temporarily obscure the road ahead of me. There was a trick to harnessing each vehicle's blinding light: I always ran with a baseball hat and while the car was about one-tenth of a mile from me, I would bow my head slightly towards the ground and let the bill of the hat block out the direct light of the car. That illuminated most of the road between the car and I, which allowed me to scan the road for hazards ahead. In this way, the occasional car passing in the darkness minimized the risk of pre-dawn running.

By the time I reached the halfway point, the skies had lightened to where the Sound on my left and the stalks of the sea oats covering the sand dunes to my right were visible. My destination was just three miles ahead and I could pick out the silhouette of the houses bordering the edge of town.

I reached Avon just after 6:00 a.m. My turnaround point was Askins Creek Store, where I went inside and purchased a 32 oz. Gatorade to rehydrate. I was drenched in sweat but feeling pretty good, having the first half of the run complete. I made sure that I stretched again before heading back, realizing that I could not avoid some soreness or stiffness once I was done. It had been a while since I covered twelve miles in a morning and my body was going to let me know about it.

The journey back to Buxton was well lit and all the oncoming traffic could see me. It was also getting warmer. However, running south on the northbound lane of Highway 12 kept me in the shadow of the ridge of sand dunes that shielded the sun's direct rays. I was good until about 7:00 a.m. After that, all bets were off.

The Beach

When I returned my wife and son were already up. I had an idea to catch a quick breakfast at the chow hall and then head to the beach. My wife agreed and so we had a delicious galley style pancake breakfast with scrambled eggs, bacon, hash browns, and a beverage, all for $1.65 per person. The chow hall was pretty empty with just a few other Coast Guardsmen eating breakfast with us.

We went back to the room to gather our gear for a most-of-the day stay on the beach. We had a couple of chairs, a cooler, blanket, towels, and a beach umbrella in the car. My wife packed the cooler with ice, juices, soft drinks, peanut butter and jelly sandwiches, and some snacks. I grabbed the rest of the gear and we walked to the edge of the station, which had a sand path through a thicket of sea oats leading out to the water. We could hear the pounding surf long before it came into view and sensed the rush of salt air it produced. All I could think about was getting the umbrella, chairs, and blanket set up so I could catch a long nap, depending on when our son was going to crash.

The Buxton shoreline

We found a spot in the sand that seemed level enough to set up camp. The trick was to get the umbrella in the perfect position—at just the right angle to block the sun and the right depth so that the ocean breezes would not blow it over. I set up my son's toddler chair, which had a high back reclining feature, my wife's chair, and then mine. I sat down and sighed, digging my feet deep into the cool sand.

Now I could finally relax!

"Hey, why don't you get into the water?" my wife asked. "The water looks great!"

"Nah, I just want to chill," I said.

She was right, though. The water was inviting, winds were warm, and the skies crystal clear. We pretty much had the beach to ourselves save the few other families dotting the shoreline and the occasional beachcomber that would pass by at the water's edge. No, I had sleep in mind. So, I moved my chair out of the shade into the direct sunlight. I sat in my chair with my ball cap off my head and tilted all the way forward to cover my entire face.

"Need some sunscreen?" my wife asked.

"Nope! I am good to go," I said.

It took me a moment but I got caught up in the sensory silence of wind, waves, and sunshine. These were my sleep aids on the beach. There was just something about the combination of these elements that was so soothing. It could help me drift off and drift away.

Ahh! Beach therapy, I thought to myself just starting to perspire under my hat. *I need more beach therapy.*

Second Morning Run

Like I predicted, I was pretty sore after my first run to Avon so I took the next day off. The next morning, I was back at it before dawn and headed north on Highway 12. It was slightly overcast as if a shower or two could be possible for later in the day. For some reason, this run made me feel detached and finally on vacation. I even caught a stretch about four miles into it where I felt a runner's high. When I reached Avon, I made my usual stop at Askins Creek Store to rehydrate.

"Good morning, Ma'am! Just this," I said to the cashier, placing a bottle of Gatorade on the counter.

"Your run going well?" she asked.

"Yes it is, thanks," I said.

"How much further do you have to go?" she asked.

"Back to Buxton, Ma'am," I said handing her two dollars.

"Buxton! You ran here from Buxton?" she asked in surprise.

"Yes, Ma'am," I said.

"Wow! That's six—No! That's twelve miles roundtrip!" she said, handing me the change.

"Yes, Ma'am. That is right," I said.

"You must be military," she said.

"Yes, Ma'am. I am in the Navy."

"Wow! Running on vacation—that is dedication!" she exclaimed.

"Yes, Ma'am. Running relaxes me and puts my mind at ease," I said.

"Running is relaxing? Huh! You *must* be military!" she said.

"Ah, Yes, Ma'am," I said with slight grin.

"Well, thank you for your service and have a good one," she said.

"You too, Ma'am," I said as I departed the store.

I had loved running since I was in junior high school, when I was on the cross country team. I have to credit the Marines, though, with *refining* my love for the discipline of running. During the three years of service with them, I put hundreds of miles on my feet running around the Mojave Desert in Twentynine Palms, CA. However, these vacation runs were about spending time with the Lord, allowing Him to speak to me and let me process "the stuff" in my heart.

Ocracoke Island

After a shower and quick breakfast, we decided to pack up the car and take the ferry over to Ocracoke Island. The drive down to the ferry took us through the rest of Buxton, the village of Frisco, and then into Hatteras Village. The distance to the ferry was only ten miles but seemed longer due to the slower speed limits along the way. In the summer, the ferry departed every half hour so there would be plenty of opportunities to go over and get back later in the day.

When we arrived at the ferry station, there was already a line of cars ahead of us waiting for the arrival of the next ferry. The custom was to put the car in park and turn it off until it was time to embark the ferry. There was a small strip mall of shops adjacent to the ferry station where we could purchase souvenirs, hats, sunglasses, towels, jewelry, ice cream, burgers—you name it! Shopping: it's what to do while waiting for the ferry. Well, people did not *have* to buy anything but it was good to have that convenience right there just in case.

Once the ferry arrived, everyone headed back to their cars and started them up. We waited a little longer to allow the cars returning from Ocracoke to debark the ferry. Then, one-by-one, the ferry attendants motioned the cars to proceed aboard the vessel. There were four lanes of parking, two outer and two inner lanes. The attendants alternated cars to either sides of the ferry filling the outer lanes first then the inside lanes last. With all the cars embarked, the ferry backed out of the slip and proceeded slowly into the channel.

"'You getting out?" asked my wife.

"Yeah, I thought I would go up to the top deck and take a look around. You want to come?" I asked.

"No. I will stay here. It is almost time for 'somebody's' lunch," my wife said looking back at our son. He was wide-awake and kicking around.

"Yeah, he looks like he has got the munchies," I said. "Okay. I won't be long up there," I said as I opened the car door.

Space was tight on the main parking deck of the ferry. I had to edge my way sideways to get anywhere on the vessel. I made my way to the ladder leading to the upper deck. There was a lounge enclosed by windows offering the best views of the channel's open waters. About midway, we encountered several small, uninhabited islands, another ferry headed in the opposite direction, as well as other private watercraft transiting the channel. Seagulls often gathered to follow the ferries across the channel, using the advancing winds to hover aloft the ferry. Once in a while, people tossed bread or chips into the air, which would cause the birds not only to swoop down and hover over the vessel but also call out to other birds in the vicinity. The gulls were wild animals capable of finding food on their own but they were also opportunists that never turned down an easy meal.

The transit took about forty-five minutes. We debarked at the direction of the attendants and headed for Ocracoke Village. It was a short trip to get there—the entire island is less than ten miles long—and once we arrived, we were welcomed by all sorts of retail shops, restaurants, art galleries, inns, bed-and-breakfasts with hand-painted signs, hanging baskets, and flower pots filled with colorful blossoms. The streets were bustling with tourists, for we were there at the height of "their season." Its charm reminded me a lot of Nantucket Island, Massachusetts.

View of the Pilot House: Ferry to Ocracoke

Ocracoke has its own lighthouse and we decided to take some family photos in front of it. In contrast to the Cape Hatteras Lighthouse, the Ocracoke Lighthouse was a quite modest eighty to ninety feet tall, gleaming-white, but in keeping with the mood and setting of the rest of the island. Over the years, I visited this lighthouse many times but the presence of my family made it a more special occasion.

After the lighthouse, we had lunch at a local restaurant and headed back to the ferry. The waiting line for the ferry returning to Hatteras Island was usually shorter than the one coming to Ocracoke. I suppose the rationale was this: Ocracoke Island was so pleasant that people did not want to leave. They stayed as long as they could even to the last ferry around midnight.

Last Morning Run

The winds were out of the northeast, which wasn't unusual. Winds across the island could come from any direction but this meant that the first half of my run would be into the wind, a more challenging way to start. The preference is to have the wind at my back or none at all. A good portion of Highway 12 between Buxton and Avon was open road and open-air, thus, it meant *I* was the windbreaker. I pushed through, though. Much of running was in my mind. If I could put my head around the distance and the elements, I could run anywhere.

I was never so glad to reach Avon and the convenience store, not so much for the pause and hydration, but for the break I was going to get from the winds on the way back. I knew I was going to get a push that would make the trip easier. When I started back, the push was immediate; I even felt faster and could now hear the sound of the crashing surf, which the head wind had all but silenced. In all, this was not the motivating run I was expecting at the end of the vacation but I made it back without a scratch.

Sand dune path to the beach

Evening Walk on the Beach

Beachcombing allowed us to discover something new every time we engaged in it: all types of people—surfers, surfcasters, swimmers, sunbathers, and other combers—and wildlife—shorebirds, scurrying sand crabs, and sea turtle nesting sites—and seashells by the thousands, strewn along the shoreline, made excellent souvenirs. The shells had variations and similarities in them all at once; in color, size, thickness, and texture; whole or fragmented. We marveled at them all but kept our favorites for ourselves.

In the fading sunlight of our last night of vacation, we took a walk on the beach along a path with no particular end point. I suppose we covered about half-of-a-mile south of the Coast Guard Station when we turned around and headed back. At the entrance of the path leading to the station, we found a family—parents with two school-aged girls—that was headed in the same direction. They had this playful small Golden Retriever puppy trudging through the sand around them. They let the puppy make his way through the sand as much as he was able but when he seemed stuck, they picked him up and placed him in a new patch.

When our paths met, I paid the family a compliment.

"What a beautiful puppy! A Golden Retriever, right?" I asked.

"Yes, he is. Just over a month old," the mother said.

"Awww! He is precious," my wife said.

I bent over to pet him and he could not stand still, circling my extending hand, wagging his tail, and licking my hands and fingers like crazy! "What loveable dog!" I said.

"Do you think your son would like to pet him?" she asked.

"Well, I guess so. A little pet on the head won't hurt." I said.

I un-strapped our son from has back carrying pack that my wife had on her back and lowered him down to puppy's level. Immediately, the puppy welcomed him with licking, sniffing, and playfulness. Unfortunately, the dog was so energetic my son became frightened. I picked him up quickly but could not prevent him from crying a little.

"Oh-oh-oh! I am *so* sorry! I am so sorry!" said the mom with anxiety. "Is he ok? I am sorry!"

"He is fine, he is fine. Just a little startled, that's all. He is fine." I said.

My son was back in my arms. "See partner, you are okay. He is just a playful little puppy," I reassured him.

"Just a little puppy. Nothing to be afraid of," my wife also reassured him.

"See, Partner, just a playful puppy." He calmed down and even cracked a smile. "'Nothing to worry about, Partner," I said.

By now, the woman picked up the puppy in her arms and brought him close to me.

"'You think he'd like to try again?" she asked.

"Yes. I will hold him and you hold the puppy. I think he will be alright," I said.

I petted the puppy first to show our son it was safe. My wife drew near and offered more encouragement.

"Go ahead, Partner. You can pet him. It is okay," I told our son. He slowly extended his arm and the woman brought the puppy up to meet his reach. Our son got in half-of-a pet on his head before the puppy began to profusely lick his hand. Our son giggled at the sensation.

"See, young man, he is a friendly little puppy," said the woman.

"Yup! Just a friendly puppy, Partner," I said. "Thanks Ma'am, for the second chance."

"No problem. I am just sorry that he startled your son," she said.

"Oh, he is fine now. Everything is okay," my wife and I reassured her.

We stepped back and let the family forge ahead on the path through the sea oats. We wished them "Good evening" and followed them close behind along the path.

"Golden Retrievers grow up to be such beautiful dogs," said my wife.

"Yeah. Beautiful! Loyal and obedient too," I said.

It was dusk when we reached our room at the lodge. After we wiped the sand from our feet and headed inside, we decided to call it an evening.

The Trip Home

I arose the next morning around five to get a head start on packing the car. I peaked outside and noticed there was a storm overnight because the streets were still wet and the parked cars had a residue of rain on them. Perhaps this would be all the rain we would get on the way back home. *It is so much better to end such a great vacation with clear skies*, I thought.

We decided to depart the lodge around 7:00 a.m. and grab breakfast on the road, perhaps in Nags Head or Kitty Hawk, by my wife made sure our son had a little something to eat before we hit road. Just as I hoped, the skies were clear to partly cloudy back up through Avon, Pea Island, and across the Bonner Bridge. The car was quiet while my wife and son both took a nap. This allowed me to soak up the last seashore scenes along the highway that had become our vacation. I passed the towering sand dunes at Jockey's Ridge State Park. When my son was old enough, I would teach him how to run right up to the edge of the tallest dune and jump, allowing him to experience the thrill of a second or two of "flight time" before a safe landing below in the soft sand. I saw the iconic Ark Church whose edifice was literally shaped like a huge ark. The Wright Brothers' Memorial with its towering granite monument commemorated the first powered plane flight. These were some of the sights that harkened back to many fond memories from earlier vacations.

Normally, locating a place to eat on the road was done by consensus. Fortunately, my wife was still asleep and I already had in mind what I wanted—pancakes! I pulled into a place called Stack 'Em High, in Kitty Hawk. My wife began to stir once I parked the car.

"We are here!" I exclaimed.

"Pancakes, again?" she asked, noticing the sign outside the restaurant.

"Yeah, sure. Why not? I wanted to give this place a try," I said.

We were not disappointed! I had the high stack—four plate-sized pancakes with maple syrup and sausage—while my wife chose the short stack. It was delicious but I was stuffed and felt like I could use another morning run to settle the account with the calories.

With a stop for gas to fill the tank and a cup of coffee from a 7-Eleven, we were on our way again. The Outer Banks came to an abrupt end as we departed Kitty Hawk and crossed over the Currituck Sound on the Wright Memorial Bridge—but not the experience. That, we carried with us long after we depart the area. In my heart, I began to recount the most recent memories from this trip and felt grateful to have had this time with my family.

The skies continued to be crystal clear and sunny on the journey. We were almost at Coinjock, North Carolina when I encouraged my wife to join our son in taking a nap. I reassured her that my coffee was still hot and would keep me company most of the way back home. Shortly after they were both sound asleep, I found an easy listening station on the radio, moved the car over to the right lane, clicked cruise control, and settled in for a peaceful ride all the way home. It was September 11th.

9/11

Nothing will ever be the same

11 September 2001
Noon

My family and I just arrived at home from a very pleasant vacation at Cape Hatteras, North Carolina. After unpacking the car, my wife and my two-year-old son remained downstairs while I headed for the bedroom to take a nap. A few moments later she burst into the bedroom and told me the unbelievable news.

America has been attacked!

She quickly turned on the television to CNN and we saw the indelible image of one of the World Trade Center towers on fire with billows of thick black smoke rising from the structure. The caption at the bottom of the screen read,

...WORLD TRADE CENTER DESTROYED IN TERRORIST ATTACK.

I thought they were mistaken because I saw only one badly damaged tower but it was still standing. Then came the replay of the second plane slamming into the South Tower.

"Oh God!" my wife gasped.

I could not believe the sheer horror I was witnessing. I shook my head in disbelief and said to her, "We are at war."

I gathered my family at the bedside for a moment of prayer. My wife looked at me and asked. "In what kind of world are we raising our son?" There was no answer I could give that would be satisfactory, for this act of terrorism was far beyond any human rationale. We bowed and prayed; tears flowed freely as we told God we had no idea what or why this was happening but only that we needed Him to bring us through.

After our prayer, I realized the military would be on high alert. I tried to call the ship to confirm what I already suspected. However, all the phone lines to the Quarterdeck were busy. I was finally able to get through to the Engineering Department. A chief petty officer answered the phone and confirmed that we had been recalled to the ship. I told my wife I had to head to the ship so I grabbed a clean set of khakis and got dressed in utter disbelief— my emotions being a mix of shock and anger. Before I left, CNN reported that as many as 50,000 people worked in the World Trade Center each day. *My goodness. Did I just see that many people die?"*

I hugged and kissed my wife and son goodbye and headed for the naval base. Every local radio station on the way was reporting on the attack in New York City and the Pentagon in Washington, DC. I was smart enough to pack some overnight items to take to the ship because I figured I would not be coming home until the following morning.

Arrival at Naval Station Norfolk

All the gate entrances to the naval station were backed up with traffic extending nearly two miles. The base's security condition had plunged from THREATCON ALPHA to DELTA. It was a slow crawl to the gate entrance due to the guards conducting a thorough search of each vehicle.

They were dressed in cammies, helmet and flak jacket, with M-16 rifles and extra ammo cartridges.

I finally made it through the gate and headed straight to the waterfront only to find all the parking spaces were taken. I had to drive to the auxiliary lot about a half mile away and walk all the way back to the waterfront. On the pier, I caught up with RP1 Bates, who informed me that SHREVEPORT, along with five other ships, had been ordered to get underway to provide support for New York City. With our regularly scheduled deployment to the Mediterranean Sea only eight days away, I began to have this sinking feeling that we were not going to come back to Norfolk but be sent straight across the Atlantic Ocean. My first thought was to try contacting my wife to tell her I was headed for New York and I was not sure when I would be back. I came aboard and dropped off my bag in my stateroom. I noticed the mood aboard ship was slightly frantic but solemn. Many sailors stood on the Mess Deck watching the aftermath of the attack on the wide-screen TV.

I could not get an open line on the ship but I knew I had to contact my wife. I decided to go the Naval Station Chapel and make the call from there. When I spoke to my wife, I told her about the news of our departure and asked her to get my extra uniforms that were at the cleaners and mail them to Naval Station in Rota, Spain—our first port visit—where I would be able to pick them up in a couple of weeks.

Getting Underway

Early that evening, the captain got on the 1MC and briefed the crew about our mission. We were going to Morehead City, North Carolina to pick up Marines and excavation equipment, then head for New York City, and stay there until we were released. After he finished, the crew continued with their underway preps. The captain called for an OPS/INTEL brief, where it was established we would be getting underway around 2100. I already began to meditate about what to say during the evening prayer and privately asked the Lord to help me say the right thing.

I took a moment to write my wife a short message to share my thoughts and give her an update on the latest developments:

From: CHAPS@SHREVEPORT
To: RB@HOME
Subject: National Day of Tragedy

Honey,

I am so hurt and disturbed that I do not know what to write. I cannot stop thinking about those who lost their lives today and their families. I am so angry with those terrorists who did this pre-meditated act. But I am glad that we prayed and affirmed our faith in the Lord before I left. Better still, I am so grateful for the wonderful vacation days down at Cape Hatteras. I really felt closer to you and our son than I ever have before. It was great just to be with family and have no agenda. Thank you so much for a wonderful time.

We are getting underway at 2100 and we will be in Morehead City by tomorrow afternoon. Then it is on to New York City to provide medical and logistical support. Personally, it will be difficult to come into New York harbor and see it without the Twin Towers. Please keep us lifted up in prayer.

I will send you more info as I receive it. Take care and God bless you!

Love,
Chaps

From: RB@HOME
To: CHAPS@SHREVEPORT
Re: National Day of Tragedy

Chaps,

This is such a difficult time for our country. I watched in horror and shock as the news reports came through the television. It is the only thing that is on just about every channel. It seems that they are finding survivors among the ruins of the towers but every minute is critical. I think they found about nine police and firemen survivors, the last I heard, this morning among the wreckage. They are estimating that possibly 850 people lost their lives in the attack on the Pentagon. No actual numbers and we may not know for some time. It is a sad day in our history—one we will never forget. The newspapers are covered with pictures of the devastation. It will take time to heal from this tragedy. We have to continue to believe that those who committed such a violent act will be brought to justice not only by man's law, but also by God's law.

The relief workers are doing all they can to save as many lives as possible. I continue to pray for those workers, the victims and their families, and for the military and for you. Be strong and continue to trust in God and His plan. I love you and we are so proud of you and what you are doing for our country.

Love,
RB

In the dark of that evening, without fanfare or family members waving from the pier, SHREVEPORT got underway to provide support and assistance to the victims of the attack.

The Evening Prayer

I arrived at the Pilot House at 2150. The sailors on Watch seemed more quiet than usual as we proceeded towards the open ocean.
"TATTOO, TATTOO! LIGHTS OUT IN FIVE MINUTES! STAND BY FOR THE EVENING PRAYER."
The Boatswain Mate-of-the-Watch handed me the microphone to the 1MC. I paused for a moment in the relative silence of the Pilot House, keyed the microphone and prayed.

National Tragedy

Let us pray.

God is our refuge and strength, a very present help in the time of trouble. Therefore, we will not be afraid though the earth is removed; though the mountains fall into the heart of the sea, though its waters roar and foam. (Psalm 46:1-3a).
O Lord, our hearts are shocked and dismayed over the terrible and tragic events of this day. You have declared in your Word: "The human heart is desperately wicked. Who can understand it?"[6] And it seems like that declaration is right on target. Right before our very eyes we witnessed the depth of depravity of the human will along with its unabashed capacity for evil.

Although the dust has not settled in any respect as to responsibility or appropriate response, SHREVEPORT has been abruptly tasked with providing whatever support is deemed necessary. O Lord, our nation needs us. Grant us the strength to serve with all diligence and care.

As we close, we remember the thousands of victims and their families. We pray for your comfort and peace to be with them in the midst of their tremendous grief and suffering. We pray for our country and our national conscience. In a situation like this we literally have to come together, pick up the pieces, and start over. Keep us focused on our mission and place a hedge of protection around our loved ones back home.

God is our refuge and strength, an ever-present help in the time of trouble. Therefore, we will not be afraid.

Amen.

---

6 Paraphrased from Jeremiah 17:9

-19-

MISSION: MOREHEAD CITY

Answering the nation's call

12 September 2001

Throughout the night and into the morning, we steamed south about thirty miles off the coast of Cape Hatteras on our way to Morehead City. When I got up, I checked my email. One of the first messages I received was from my brother.

From: JAB@HOME
To: CHAPS@SHREVEPORT
Subject: Trade Center Attack

Hey Dave,

Don't know what to say this time out. First thing is I hope whatever duties or functions you are asked to perform are done without any further bloodshed or loss of life. I know the military has been put on high alert and some of the Atlantic Fleet is sailing for the New York City area.

Just praying for *all* that lost their lives, their families and loved ones, and to those who are struggling to save, rescue, and secure the area. Just want you to know I am praying for you, your family, and those you are with during these troubled and desperate times.

Take care, be well, and return home safely!

Love,
JAB

From: CHAPS@SHREVEPORT
To: JAB@HOME
Re: Trade Center Attack

Hey Bro!

Thanks for your prayers and concern. As you already know we are one of the ships headed for New York to provide logistical and medical support for the victims.

What a terrible thing was this attack! This is our generation's Pearl Harbor. I spent most of the day shocked and deeply disturbed. My wife and I took the time to pray before I went back to work because I was not sure what was going to happen once I got on base. It seems as though we will be up in New York City for about five days, maybe more, then hopefully come back for a few days, then head across the Atlantic.

If you have a chance, please give my wife a call. I know it will encourage her to hear from family. Thanks again for reaching out. Tell everyone I said, "Hi" and that I am doing fine.

Love,
Dave

From: CHAPS@SHREVEPORT
To: RB@HOME
Subject: The Day After

Honey,

I am feeling a little bit better than I did yesterday. Everything was such an emotional roller coaster that it was hard to catch up with my responsibilities. I had looked forward to a day of relaxation to prepare for coming to work today but it was not meant to be. I did not want to leave you and our son like that but I am glad and grateful that you understood and were supportive.

When I got up this morning, I headed straight for the Pilot House to see how far south we had traveled. As I opened the hatch and looked out across the sea, I saw what I thought was Chesapeake Light (called CHESLIGHT), which is located at the mouth of the Chesapeake Bay right outside of Virginia Beach. Immediately I thought we had been "cutting squares" in the ocean all night and I became disappointed that we had not progressed any further. Derby Luckie was the OOD and I asked him why we were still by CHESLIGHT. He told me that it was Hatteras Light (HATLIGHT?) and that we were off the coast of Kitty Hawk, North Carolina. I was silent and thought to myself, *just twenty-four hours ago we were sitting down and having a breakfast right about this spot.* What a difference a day makes!

My brother sent me an encouraging email this morning. I told him I was doing fine and to tell everyone I said, "Hi."

I miss you both very much. I had such a great time on vacation. I will talk to you again soon.

Love,
Chaps

From: RB@HOME
To: CHAPS@SHREVEPORT
Re: The Day After

Chaps,

I continue to see those images from yesterday's attack and it is just hard to believe that it happened. My grandmother called and she is fine. She said some of the smoke and debris flew over into Brooklyn. It looks like the buildings around the World Trade Center are somewhat unstable. I believe part of one building next door to the WTC collapsed today. The toll at the Pentagon is estimated about one hundred to two hundred not eight hundred as originally estimated. I heard reports that the wing of the building that was hit was the Navy side and I do not know if they have found survivors. Have you heard anything? This is so totally devastating for the entire nation.

Continue to pray for healing and for our nation, for the families of the victims, and for the world.

God bless you!
RB

As we continued to sail for Morehead City, I felt a need to inform my Church of our involvement in the crisis. The best point of contact would be Chaplain Calvin Sydnor, a retired Army chaplain and a professor of religion and ethics at Hampton University. He always did an excellent job keeping our church informed about the latest news regarding military chaplaincy.

From: CHAPS@SHREVEPORT
To: CHSYDNOR@HU
Subject: Headed to New York City

Chaplain Sydnor,

As you know, the entire military has been placed on full alert in response to the attack on the World Trade Center in New York City. My ship, the USS SHREVEPORT (LPD-12), and Chaplain Valcourt's, the USS VELLA GULF (CG-72), have been directed to go to New York Harbor to provide logistical, medical, and air defense support. Just thought you and our church should know that AME chaplains are "On Point" to provide pastoral ministry support to the victims, their families, and to the emergency medical teams. Currently, my ship is headed south to Morehead City, North Carolina to pick up some Marines and then we will turn toward New York. Chaplain Valcourt will arrive in New York Harbor today. Please pass the word to our colleagues, soliciting their prayers as we are called to minister in this crisis situation.

Very respectfully,
Chaplain Brown

STANDOWN: RETURN TO NORFOLK

The mission changes

13 September 2001
From: CHAPS@SHREVEPORT
To: RB@HOME
Subject: Awaiting Further Instructions

Good Morning!

We are pier side in Morehead City and we are waiting for further instructions from higher headquarters. No one knows anything for sure, though. Please be patient and keep praying for us. I am doing very well, Praise the Lord! I have a great network of Christian brothers on the ship to keep me encouraged. Also, the emails you forward from others help too so keep sending any info from home. Right now, you are the best and most accurate source of information. Please keep sending what you know whenever you get the chance. Again, we are awaiting a movement order to head to New York City. It seems like this is just the beginning of a drawn-out process.

From: RB@HOME
To: CHAPS@SHREVEPORT
Re: Awaiting Further Instructions

I spoke with my mom and dad and your brother. Everyone is still in shock over the tragic events but we are doing okay. I am saving the newspapers this week. I thought you would be interested in the news coverage of the attack.

Did you know that the president declared tomorrow, Friday, as a National Day of Prayer and Remembrance for the victims and families? Are you going to do something special on the ship?

There is nothing else to report from this end. Take care and know that our thoughts and prayers are with you and your shipmates as well.

Love,
RB

From: CHAPS@SHREVEPORT
To: CHAPLAIN@PHIBGRU2
Subject: General Update

Good Morning Sir!

Here is what I know about our operation:

We arrived in Morehead City and are on standby for the next six hours, waiting to receive further instructions. We are not sure if our support for New York City will be "Go" or "No-go" but no one feels this is an exercise in futility. We all know why we are here and are anxious to get started. Also, we are still waiting on our Marine support assets to arrive.

Here is what I sense from the crew:

As I conducted deckplate ministry, every Sailor asked me how long we were going to be out and if we were going back to Norfolk before we head across the sea. It seems that the trauma of getting underway with little or no notice had many thinking, *what's next?* The news reports that keep flooding the TV have the sailors wondering what they will be tasked to do once they get there. Our embarked assets have a pretty clear mission upon arrival. However, the same cannot be said for the sailors. Some officers have expressed that the more they see on TV, the less they want to go and see it first-hand. I am listening and talking to everyone who wants to share. The crew senses we are being pulled into something bigger than we have been trained.

Here is what I suspect:

There already exists a need for Critical Incident Stress Debriefing (CISD) teams to be on hand in New York City. I fear rescue workers will begin to collapse, break down, or incur other health repercussions due to the extreme stress of this crisis. If we get there and sailors, either voluntarily or through tasking, get involved we will require stress debriefing too.

As for me, I have a host of good Christian brothers to talk with and an inner circle to unload my burdens. I have already visited the doctor just to keep that line of support open. Please continue to pray for us all.

Thanks for your support!

V/r,
Chaplain Brown

From: CHAPLAIN@PHIBGRU2
To: CHAPS@SHREVEPORT
Re: General Update

Chaplain Brown,

Still do not know what is next, but I hope you will come back to port to bid farewell to your loved ones prior to deployment.

Recommend that you start training teams within the SHREVEPORT family in CISD. Regardless of where you are or will be sent in the future, this is an important baseline requirement for any military unit that regularly goes into harm's way.

Will write more soon when I have better information.

Blessings,
PHIBGRU2 Chaplain

It took about eight hours to get the news that we had been ordered to standown and return to Norfolk. Apparently, more than enough search and rescue resources had reached Manhattan and our services were no longer required. Ironically, this news brought a sense of relief to the crew because we were all convinced we were heading straight across the Atlantic right after New York.

Sometime after dinner, I heard over the 1MC:
"CHAPLAIN BROWN, YOUR PRESENCE IS REQUESTED IN THE CAPTAIN'S CABIN."

The captain called me to his cabin to offer some advice for this evening's prayer. Although he had never done so before, he suggested I craft something that would tell the crew the deployment, less than a week away, had already begun. I sensed he was concerned the crew might lose their mission focus and revert to a standown state-of-mind. I took his request under advisement and did my best to accommodate his wishes.

Pilot House
2155
"TATTOO, TATTOO! LIGHTS OUT IN FIVE MINUTES! STAND BY FOR THE EVENING PRAYER."

Gather and Continue

Gracious Lord, as we return home, we thank you that we were ready to answer the call to support our fellow Americans in the midst of the crisis. Although we did not have the chance to lend a hand, we thank you for the countless hands and hearts of the American people who have shown their resilience and resourcefulness through their rescue and recovery efforts. Bless them with the courage and strength to carry on.

Lord, you have called us to a different path.

You have called us to gather our belongings and ourselves. To restack our priorities and even redeem lost time—time to take care of all the in-port and at-home responsibilities, those last minute details and honey-do lists that await us in Norfolk.

You have called us to continue the good work begun in Fort Lauderdale, Antigua, New York, Norfolk, and even all the way to the Mediterranean. Continue to turn stumbling blocks into stepping-stones just as we have done throughout FEP, JTFX, and most certainly in all future operations.

Lord, as we sail home to gather and continue our journey across the sea, surround us with your Spirit, protect us with your love, and bless us with your favor.

All this we ask in your Holy Name.
Amen.

EPILOGUE

*C*ontinue the Journey! In "Spirit Soundings Volume II: The Patriot's Call", Chaplain David Reid Brown, Commander, U.S. Navy (Ret.) shares his poignant account of the perils of a wartime deployment to Afghanistan, our nation's first in support of Operation Enduring Freedom. Follow the crew of the USS SHREVEPORT as they head into the unknowns of a combat environment.

Finish the Journey! In "Spirit Soundings Volume III: The Return to America", Chaplain David Reid Brown, Commander, U.S. Navy (Ret.) concludes this inspirational story with the heartfelt account of homecoming to America. Follow the crew of the USS SHREVEPORT as they diligently work their way home to a hero's welcome.

ABOUT THE AUTHOR

David Reid Brown is an Itinerant Elder in the African Methodist Episcopal Church and a retired Navy Chaplain with twenty-one years of Active Duty service. He is preparing to plant a church, *Hale Ho'onani* ("House of Praise") *Fellowship,* on the Windward side of the island of O'ahu, Hawaii. He is also pursing a Master's Degree in Education with an aspiration of becoming a schoolteacher.